Praise for
The Walk

"I have profound respect for people who are better in person than they are in public. That is Shaun Alexander. He doesn't just talk the talk; he walks the walk. And that is what this book is all about."

> —MARK BATTERSON, best-selling author of *In a Pit with a Lion on a Snowy Day*

"Shaun Alexander is an inspiration to those going through the 'walk' that we call our daily lives. His insight and wisdom will cause readers to look deep inside and seek after God. His candor and spiritual maturity teach us how to live happier, more purpose-filled lives. Once you start reading this book, you won't be able to put it down."

> —MATTHEW BARNETT, senior pastor of the Dream Center

"*The Walk* is a must-read for anyone who has questions about faith or who wonders what it would be like to have a more tangible relationship with God. It presents a picture of God we can connect with every day. From math tests to touchdowns, Shaun's incredible insights and personal stories will give you the practical tools you need to navigate through life's biggest challenges."

> —ERICA GREVE, minister and conference speaker

"Shaun Alexander has been a model and a blessing to countless young people in the Communities In Schools program, offering students hope for a future. When Shaun writes about those who are Examples—'people who actually live what they claim to believe'—I see his face and hear his voice."

> —BILL MILLIKEN, founder and vice-chairman of Communities In Schools Inc. and author of *The Last Dropout* and *Tough Love*

"Ever since I first met Shaun at the Senior Bowl, I have been impressed by his consistency, his humility, and his teachable spirit. I have watched him mature as he has learned to live out his faith. This book will take you through some of the same steps he took in that growth process, and I know you will be challenged and blessed."

—CAREY CASEY, CEO of the National Center for Fathering and author of *Championship Fathering*

"Shaun lives with integrity and honor in the public eye. But it's the life he lives when no one is watching that amazes us. His relationship with God and intimate knowledge of the Scriptures have given him a strong foundation for his entire life. With *The Walk,* Shaun makes these insights available to people of all walks of life in order to deepen their walk with God."

—JOHN and LISA BEVERE, authors, international speakers, and cofounders of Messenger International

"The greatness of Shaun Alexander running downfield with a football is but a glimpse of the greatness he walks in without a football. This man of God has written a phenomenal book that can spark the greatness in all of us. *The Walk* will allow us to start our walk toward a much better world, right from where we are."

—MICHAEL JR., Christian comedian

SHAUN ALEXANDER

WITH JOE HILLEY

Clear Direction and

Spiritual Power

for Your Life

THE
WALK

WATERBROOK
PRESS

THE WALK
PUBLISHED BY WATERBROOK PRESS
12265 Oracle Boulevard, Suite 200
Colorado Springs, Colorado 80921

All Scripture quotations, unless otherwise indicated, are taken from the Holy Bible, New International Version®. NIV®. Copyright © 1973, 1978, 1984 by Biblica Inc.™ Used by permission of
Zondervan. All rights reserved worldwide. www.zondervan.com. Scripture quotations marked
(RSV) are taken from the Revised Standard Version of the Bible, copyright © 1952 [2nd edition,
1971] by the Division of Christian Education of the National Council of the Churches of Christ
in the USA. Used by permission. All rights reserved.

Italics in Scripture quotations reflect the author's added emphasis.

Details in some anecdotes and stories have been changed to protect the identities of the persons
involved.

ISBN 978-0-307-45951-0
ISBN 978-0-307-45952-7 (electronic)

Published in the United States by WaterBrook Multnomah, an imprint of the Crown Publishing
Group, a division of Random House Inc., New York.

WATERBROOK and its deer colophon are registered trademarks of Random House Inc.

Library of Congress Cataloging-in-Publication Data
Alexander, Shaun.
  The walk : clear direction and spiritual power for your life / Shaun Alexander with Joe Hilley.
  — 1st ed.
      p. cm.
  Includes bibliographical references.
  ISBN 978-0-307-45951-0 — ISBN 978-0-307-45952-7 (electronic)
  1. Christian life. 2. Spiritual formation. 3. Maturation (Psychology)—Religious aspects—
Christianity. I. Hilley, Joe. II. Title.
  BV4501.3.A436 2010
  248.4—dc22
                          2010015102

Printed in the United States of America
2010—First Edition

10 9 8 7 6 5 4 3 2 1

SPECIAL SALES
Most WaterBrook Multnomah books are available at special quantity discounts when
purchased in bulk by corporations, organizations, and special-interest groups. Custom
imprinting or excerpting can also be done to fit special needs. For information, please e-mail
SpecialMarkets@WaterBrookMultnomah.com or call 1-800-603-7051.

I heard the Holy Spirit say,
"This is what happens when you walk
the Walk. Not perfection. I'm not looking
for perfection. I'm looking for order."

—Shaun Alexander

Contents

PART 6: Walking the Walk

There are Bible heroes who stand out in your memory, typically the warriors, emancipators, and martyrs that you learned about in Sunday school. Or in my case, from aunts and uncles who told me these amazing stories at family functions and get-togethers.

Then there are biblical heroes who were just as faithful in serving God, but their names aren't on the tip of anybody's tongue. Enoch, for example, doesn't attract a lot of attention. He didn't get swallowed by a great fish, nor did he sling a rock at a giant to save his nation. And he never heard a voice talking from inside a burning bush.

But when talk turns to walking with God, you can't do better than Enoch. He is a man who, technically, didn't die. It's true that he left earth and went to heaven, but unlike the rest of humanity (except Elijah; see 2 Kings 2:11), Enoch didn't die first. The writer of Genesis doesn't make a big deal out of it but says only that Enoch "was no more, because God took him away" (5:24).

Aside from not dying, Enoch was known for enjoying an excessively long life. But even that is not the thing that stands out when you read the brief account of the centuries he spent on earth. What stands out is this: "Enoch *walked with God 300 years*" (Genesis 5:22). Think about that. For three centuries, Enoch kept walking with God. And after they walked together, God "took him away."

For Enoch, the last step he took on earth was probably nothing special. I imagine it was a lot like stepping out the front door of his house or stepping over one of his great-great-great-great-great-great-great-great-

great-grandchildren napping on the living room floor. Enoch's first step into heaven was a step a lot like any other he had taken, because this man already had been walking with God for *centuries*.

THE IMPORTANCE OF WALKING

When you read the Bible, you see that God has been big on walking from the start. After Adam and Eve disobeyed Him, they heard "the sound of the LORD God as he was walking in the garden in the cool of the day" (Genesis 3:8). When they hid from God, He called to them. And soon after that, God sacrificed an animal to provide skins as a covering for their nakedness. It is the first record in Scripture of a blood sacrifice being used to address the sin of humanity.

The more we read in the Bible about walking, the more we realize that it's best done with someone else. It's not easy to walk alone. It's not even easy to stand alone. The writer of Ecclesiastes points out that "if one falls down, his friend can help him up. But pity the man who falls and has no one to help him up!" (4:10). When Jesus went to the Garden of Gethsemane to pray on the night of His betrayal and arrest, He begged His closest friends to keep watch with Him. He knew He would soon be walking into the most painful ordeal anyone has ever faced, and He didn't want to walk there alone. Sadly, His disciples failed Him and fell asleep.

God, however, is a faithful Walking Companion. It's no accident that Scripture often characterizes the life of faith as a life of "walking with God." A number of biblical luminaries, Enoch included, are described as people who walked with God. Noah was an early Believer who walked with God (see Genesis 6:9). Abraham was called the friend of God (see James 2:23). In Psalms and Proverbs we read promises of blessing (see Psalm 84:11 as one example) and sure footing (see Proverbs 10:9) directed at those who walk uprightly. Jacob, after spending a night wrestling with an angel, was given a new name (Israel) and a new limp (see Genesis 32:25, 28, 31). He was able to walk afterward but with a noticeable catch in his step. From then on, as Jacob moved through life, the way he walked called attention to his time of wrestling with God.

Moses, the greatest leader and lawgiver of the Jews, spent a lifetime learning what it takes to get from Point A to Point B. He walked with God through Egypt's halls of power, then across obscure hills, where he tended sheep for forty years, and then across the Sinai wilderness for another forty years as he led the Hebrews from slavery to freedom. Moses completed eighty years of hard walking *after* he was deposed as prime minister of Egypt. He was familiar with fame and power as well as anonymity. Moses walked with God for decades and was known as the meekest man on earth (see Numbers 12:3).

Noah walked with God and built an ark that rescued the human population and the animal kingdom from a worldwide flood. At God's direction, Abraham walked out of his home country and, with his wife, gave birth to the new nation that God was creating. Moses, after herding sheep and then returning to Egypt, freed approximately two million Jews from bondage. And as we noted already, Enoch walked with God for three hundred years and disappeared into heaven without a trace.

Ark builder, father of a nation, the meekest man on earth, faithful companion of God, and a tenacious wrestler who walked away from a bout with God bearing a limp. They knew what it meant to walk with God, and the things they learned as they walked are the same things you and I need in our lives. If we hope to find a life that rises above doubt and confusion, that is enriched by order and clear direction, and that enjoys the presence, blessing, and power of God, we need to first learn how to walk with God.

THE POWER OF THREE WORDS

To hear people talk about it, you'd think the phrase "walking with God" contained only two words: *walking* and *God*. Preachers love to talk about the walking part. "You gotta keep moving ahead." "God can't steer a parked car." "You're losing ground unless you're moving forward." "If you don't keep walking, you'll never get anywhere." And my personal favorite: "Two-thirds of *God* is *go*."

Also there is always a preacher or Bible teacher who reminds us that walking, by itself, won't get things done when it comes to the Christian life. The biggest key to the life of faith is God, of course.

When a Christian thinks about walking with God, it's clear there are many variables included in that walk: when, where, how, and who can come with you. No matter what you do or the goals you have, God is our most important Walking Partner. And there is a very practical reason why this is important. Your Walking Companion determines the destination of your life. Walk with God, and you'll live in His will. But walk with money and possessions, and you might get them or you might not. But one thing is sure: you'll never be satisfied with them, and you'll crave more.

Walk with the pleasures of the flesh, and they might excite you for a moment. But the ending is the same. Walk with recognition and accomplishment, and you might get a certificate to hang on your wall. But just like money and the pleasures of the flesh, fame and accomplishment leave after the excitement fades. Then you will be left wanting more.

So decide now that you will walk with God, and you'll learn more about the things of God and what He wants for your life.

The word in the middle

As you walk with God, don't overlook the word in the middle of the phrase "walking with God." Noah and Enoch and Abraham, Jacob and

Moses, and a much larger cloud of witnesses knew that God calls us to walk *with* Him. When you explore this way of life, you realize how easy it is to miss that link, which is that God invites us to walk *with* Him. The preposition is important.

We all need to pay close attention to the position of the walker (you and me) relative to our Companion (God) as we walk with Him. Read the Bible, and you'll see men and women, old and young, walking *with* God. Ruth walked out of her familiar homeland. Esther walked into the forbidden court of the king. Stephen walked in front of the religious zealots who were ready to stone him. The Samaritan woman walked to the well to draw Jesus a drink of water.

So don't stop walking. And when you walk, don't walk away from God or ahead of Him or lag behind Him. Walk *with* God. Jesus told His disciples that He would no longer call them servants, but friends. "You are my friends if you do what I command" (John 15:14). "I have called you friends, for everything that I learned from my Father I have made known to you" (John 15:15). Jesus trusted His friends with the knowledge of God, the teachings He had received from His Father. Good friends trust one another, talk together, and walk together. Much of the teaching that Jesus is referring to, the teachings He imparted to His disciples, was done when they were walking together from Galilee to Jerusalem and elsewhere.

YOUR NEXT STEP

If you ask people to tell you the biggest questions they have about God, it's best to wait until they get past their initial issues. Often they will begin with "Why would a loving God allow suffering?" and "Will the pagans living in remote regions of the world who never heard about Jesus have a chance to get into heaven?" But then they will start to talk about the issues that are most personal to them. They will raise questions that they live with every day, things like:

- Why doesn't God speak to me?
- Why isn't God helping me figure out what to do with my life?
- Why is God's direction in my life so unclear?
- Why is it so hard for me to trust God with my life?
- Why am I here, and what am I supposed to be doing?
- Why is it so difficult to do the right thing?
- Why does my life feel empty?

At some point we all have asked ourselves, or God, most of those questions. The questions aren't a problem; it's the answers we settle for that can trip us up. We know we need to walk with God, but it's easy to misplace the emphasis. We tend to think it's all about how perfectly we walk or how fast or how far we can walk. We think of it as a contest or competition, something we do to impress God with our righteousness and commitment. The truth is, God isn't looking for perfection, and you'll never be able to walk fast enough to impress Him.

Remember the overlooked preposition *with*. For many of us, walking *with* God gets twisted into running ahead of God, or dragging our feet when we sense God wants us to change our life, or arguing against where God wants us to go. None of these has a thing to do with the type of walking that Noah and Enoch were known for.

When you walk with God, you don't try to elbow Him out of the way so you can concentrate on your own agenda, and you don't attempt to talk God into taking a different path—one that is more to your liking or style. Instead, you walk *with* Him, and that is what will give your life a rhythm, plus God's direction and order. It's a life full of power and unknown moments that you will gladly embrace.

WALKING WITH GOD OR RUNNING A RACE?

Maybe you're a Type A individual who has trouble sitting still. You eat dinner while standing up. You watch the late news while reading CNN online and tweeting about it. You set up business appointments over the phone while applying mascara as you drive to work. You go through your e-mail in-box while you return phone calls and read text messages. Maybe the idea of walking with God sounds like the most boring life you can imagine. Walking is slow, while your life is on the fast track. So who has time for it? Plus, didn't Paul say a lot about running the race?

He did, and no one ran the race better than Paul. He also knew the race lasts a lifetime. Enoch finished his race after three hundred years of walking.

We need a Pacesetter, because there is so much that comes at us in life. Jesus called His disciples friends, and they walked together. Abraham was known as God's friend, and Abraham walked out of his old life into a new life that God had promised him. Noah built a huge ship on dry land, far from the nearest body of water that could accommodate it. Moses was the number-two man in the government of the most powerful nation on the planet, and his next career move was to watch sheep in a Middle Eastern backwater.

Mary got pregnant before she was married, even though she'd never had sex. Jeremiah was abandoned in a cistern. David killed a giant and later lived in a palace, but he also was hunted by a homicidal king. Solomon asked for wisdom and received it; Job lost everything he had and then gained God; John the Baptist lost his head; and John the apostle knew the tender love of Jesus.

Walking might seem slow, but it's the biggest adventure you'll ever undertake.

GOD'S ORDER FOR YOUR LIFE

God told us in advance how He will work in our lives, and while the details vary from one person to the next, the general pattern is always the same. God leads us, teaches us, and deepens us through five stages of spiritual maturity. He works in us even before we trust Him with our lives, speaking to us while we are still Unbelievers. He keeps walking with us when we become Believers to teach and train us so that we can grow to live as Examples. He works with Examples to build them and disciple them to one day explain to others why they live the way they do. That is when Examples grow into Teachers. God then calls some Teachers to become Imparters, doing the miraculous work of Jesus on earth.

As we walk, we will encounter unexpected adventures, and we'll get involved in things we never dreamed we'd be doing. We'll walk through things that are painful, confusing, difficult, inspiring, miraculous, and glorious. At times we will walk with God in obscurity, through long periods of preparation. Later we will walk with Him in times of high visibility and heavy responsibility. If it sounds daunting and like more than you're prepared for, remember the key. Always the key is to walk *with* God.

In this book we will study God, who is a God of order and who promises to bring purpose, power, and direction to our lives. And we'll study what the Walk looks like. As Moses found out, sometimes walking with God means being an infant left in a willow basket floating in the Nile. Sometimes it looks like serving as prime minister of the number-one world power. At other times it looks suspiciously like sitting alone in a field, staring at sheep.

If you are living at God's pace and according to His order, your life will take on a rhythm that no other life can deliver. God is not out to make you famous. Instead, He wants to make you a success at hearing His voice and doing His will. Let's begin the Walk.

CHAPTER 1

The Walk

All through history, people have asked,
"Is there anything not possible?"

—SHAUN ALEXANDER

Sweat drips from my nose as I lean over, hands on my knees, and gasp for breath. I look across the huddle at the left tackle. He's a high school all-state pick; he's a college all-American; he's an all-pro offensive lineman in the National Football League (NFL). Our eyes meet, and I grin at him. He nods back as if to say, "Follow me."

To my right is the fullback. Blood trickles down his forearm, and mud covers his jersey, but he doesn't seem to mind. He's my running mate and my protector. He leads the way, opening holes in the line and throwing his body against linebackers, safeties, and defensive ends who try to stop me. He catches my eye and winks as if to say, "Let's do it."

Moments later the quarterback leans into the huddle. "All right. We need two yards for a first down. Green, power right, check, shift right, F left, ninety-seven OT on two." This is a play where I follow the fullback to the right through a hole between the right guard and the right tackle.

As we break the huddle, I see the crowd stand to its feet. At the far end of the field, the American flag flaps in the breeze. The crowd is cheering, watching, hoping. Seven yards behind the line of scrimmage, knees bent, cleats digging into the turf, I ease into position.

And then everything slows down—the American flag on its pole, the crowd, the players on the field. As if in slow motion, linemen settle into their stance, planting their hands in the grass. Tension fills the air. Something big is about to happen. The quarterback barks the signals, firm and decisive. "Set. Hut!"

Suddenly there's a loud pop as our linemen collide with players on the defensive line. Up and down the line of scrimmage, groaning and growling, players wrestle like gladiators. As the quarterback drops back, I step to the right. In the next instant I feel the ball slap against my stomach. I clutch it with both arms. My legs are moving, my mind racing. Read it. Read it. Hit the hole or cut back. "Cut!" I plant my foot and explode through the line.

Ahead of me, the fullback crashes into a linebacker. The slot receiver sprints toward the safety. As they collide, the safety flips into the air.

The crowd gasps.

With the safety out of the way, I move to the left toward the sideline. From the corner of my eye, I catch a glimpse of the crowd on its feet. Fans are waving their arms and screaming, but all I hear is the *whoow, whoow, whoow* of my breath as I sprint down the field.

By then the cornerback has taken an angle on me and is closing fast. He cuts into my lead with every step. I run harder and harder, calling on every ounce of strength in my body, past the forty-yard line, then the thirty, and the twenty. The cornerback is closing the gap as my foot crosses the ten-yard line. I can hear him behind me and just to the right. I can feel his eyes boring in on me and know that every muscle in his body is pushing to knock me down.

At the five-yard line he dives, reaching with both hands to make the tackle. His arms brush my cleats. I stumble, put my hand on the ground, then stumble again. All the while I tell myself, *Pick up your head.* As I stagger to the right, I lift my chin. My feet come under me, and I sweep into the end zone for a touchdown. A sixty-yard run on third-and-two. Now that's what I'm talking about!

The roar of the crowd echoes in my helmet as I turn to celebrate with my teammates. Then up the field I see the trainer and members of my team running toward the thirty-yard line. A player is lying on the ground, writhing in pain. I jog up the field and join the players who are gathered around him. I can see that his leg is broken, twisted at a sickening angle.

"Get the cart," someone orders. Others sigh with resignation, knowing an injury like that could take a player out of the game for the remainder of the season, perhaps even for good.

Then, without hesitation, some of us kneel beside our injured teammate. We lay our hands on his leg and begin to pray, invoking God's healing presence and power. We agree together, just as Scripture says, "Lord, let Your will be done here on earth, as it is in heaven. There are no broken bones in heaven" (see Matthew 6:9–10). As we pray, the player's shattered bone moves back into place, perfectly aligned and as strong as before. Our teammate looks up at us, his eyes wide with wonder.

How would you express the feeling of having your broken leg repaired by God while you're lying on a football field?

By then the crowd is silent, many standing with their hands to their faces in a look of amazement. They start to murmur, and the look on their faces says they have never seen anything like this. Even those of us who prayed for our teammate to be healed watch in awe as he trots toward the sideline. I turn to the others, look at them, and point to—

Just then my eyes popped open, and I stared at the ceiling. My heart was pounding. "It was just a dream," I whispered. I glanced at the alarm clock and rubbed my eyes. "But couldn't it really happen, just like that?"

I have dreamed that dream many times, wearing the different uniforms of the teams I've been a part of in high school, college, and the NFL, and I have realized that I'm not really me in that dream. I represent a Christian who believes in God's power and lives in such a way that God is free to work through his life. The dream illustrates what God can do through a life that is fully yielded and obedient to Him.

Still, I ask myself, is it possible? Can God do today what He did long ago through men like Moses, Elijah, and the first-century apostles? Is it possible for us to experience His miraculous presence to the same extent they did? I think it is. Scripture certainly suggests that it's possible. But how?

LIVING YOUR DREAM

Football has been more than a dream for me. I began playing as a young boy, back in Florence, Kentucky. With the help of coaches, my parents, and many others, I developed skills as a player and earned a football scholarship to the University of Alabama. There, I played for Coach Gene Stallings and Mike Dubose with the Crimson Tide. After college I was drafted in the first round (nineteenth overall) to play for the Seattle Seahawks.

My sixth season with the Seahawks was my breakout year. I set a number of team and NFL records[1] and was named the NFL's Most Valuable Player. At the conclusion of that season, we won the National Football Conference championship and went to the Super Bowl. Although we lost to Pittsburgh, that season was one of my best ever.

As I began my seventh season in 2006, I looked forward to building on what we'd accomplished the prior year. I trained hard and came to the season's first game with great expectations. We opened that year against the Detroit Lions.

Sometimes life-changing events come to you with a sign written in huge letters that spell out "Your Life Is About to Change." Other times the moment slips by with little or no recognition. That game against

Detroit was one of the latter. I didn't realize its significance until months afterward.

During that game a defensive lineman fell on my foot, pinning it in place between his body and the ground. He had shot through the line toward me, and as I cut left to escape his grasp, one of his teammates met me face to face. All three of us fell to the ground. This seemed like a normal play: you get the ball, you run, you get tackled. Pads crash, bodies hit the turf, the whistle blows, everybody gets up and tries it again. That's football. That's normal.

But on this play my left foot got sandwiched between the ground and the lineman's three-hundred-pound body. As I trotted back to the huddle, I could feel the pain.

For a football player, physical pain is a way of life. Since I began playing organized football as a young boy, I have taken the field while nursing sprains, strains, and aches in almost every part of my body. That day against Detroit I didn't think about the pain. But the pain in my foot never went away. I continued to play that day and carried the ball nineteen times for fifty-one yards. The pain was a distraction, and I failed to gain the yardage that I expected of myself, but I wasn't too concerned.

After the game team doctors told me I had a bone bruise. That's a medically nonspecific term for "You got hit hard, and the pain goes to the bone." I spent time with the trainer but continued to play. Two weeks later, in a game against the New York Giants, the bruise became a fracture, and I was out most of the season.

Doctors told me to stay off my foot, so I spent a lot of time reading. One of the books I read goes deep into the reality of spiritual warfare.[2] While reading *The Call* by Rick Joyner, I realized that God works in an orderly fashion; He is a God of order. And as I listened to God, I saw that some things in my life were out of order.

MEETING THE GOD OF ORDER

I've been a Christian since I was ten years old. Loving Jesus has been the center of my life. As important as football has been, it has always been second to following the Lord and allowing Him to work His will through me. As I read Joyner's book, God spoke to me about how He uses order to bring about His will.

Through the remainder of the NFL season, I continued to do exercises to rehab my injured foot, preparing to return to the game. All the while God was speaking to me about the importance of His order. He doesn't do things haphazardly. As the Scriptures tell us, God is not a God of confusion or disorder (see 1 Corinthians 14:33). And much more than simply an interesting idea, God's order became something I felt compelled to apply to my life.

With the Holy Spirit as my Guide, I allowed God to review my friends and relationships, and I started to put people—and especially business relationships—into their proper places. I stopped associating with some of the people I had considered friends and began associating with others I had been neglecting. I discontinued some of the business deals I'd been involved in. At the same time I began to pay closer attention to the things I said, particularly the half truths I would sometimes say in casual conversation or in encouraging others.

I finished that NFL season well. My second game back I had a forty-carry, 200-yard game on Monday Night Football. The Seahawks won the division and were headed to the play-offs. We lost in the divisional play-off game against the Chicago Bears in overtime. I gained 120 yards combined and scored two touchdowns in our losing effort. After missing several games and coming back to finish the season, I was excited about the next year.

The following year my foot was healed, and I looked forward to playing a full season. I performed well through training camp and the pre-season games. Then, in the first game of the regular season, I bobbled a pass. As I dove to catch it, I fell on my arm and broke my left wrist. Team doctors put my wrist and hand in a cast, and I continued to play, but the cast did little to protect my broken wrist. The weight of it actually caused additional pain, and I struggled to get past that injury. Additional injuries nagged at me for the remainder of the season.

For the fifth year in a row the Seahawks went to the play-offs. We won the division title for the fourth consecutive year. I was happy for the team, but personally I had a year that fell well short of what I expected. The bruises, strains, and broken bones were adding up, and I wondered if they were a signal. Was God using the pain in my body to prepare me mentally and emotionally for a shift to a new stage in my life?

As the following spring approached, I sensed something was going on with the team. Changes were in the wind, but I didn't know what the changes might bring. Then, as the time for spring conditioning camp approached, the Seahawks' managers called me. "We're making changes. We want to take a different direction. We're releasing you from the team." And just like that, I was out of the NFL.

Aside from my desire to love and serve God, football had been the primary focus of my life. It was the means God had used to lift me from the small town of Florence, Kentucky, to a life that few athletes ever experience. But I never lost sight of the fact that God—and not the Seattle Seahawks or the University of Alabama or Boone County High School back home—was the One who was blessing me. God is the Source of all goodness and beauty, all truth and love, and it was His favor that took me to the places I'd gone, even to the discouraging day when the Seahawks let me go. I had things I still wanted to do as a football player, but I said, "God's will be done," and went home to find out what that would mean.

A NEW WAY OF WALKING

Over the next few months, I wrestled with a new direction for my career and my life. During that time God challenged me. "Meet Me at five in the morning. Let's talk for an hour, every day." That was a wonderful invitation. The Creator of the universe wanted to spend an hour with me every day. I was excited about it, but there was a problem. He wanted to meet me in the morning. At five o'clock.

Reading the Bible has always been important to me. When I was younger, I read because that was what I was told to do. Later I realized Scripture was a powerful tool God could use in my life. Once I understood that, I began to read and study every day. I prayed every day, too, some days almost constantly, but I heard the voice of God speaking to me more when I read the Scriptures. So I was eager to meet with Him every day, even though I am not a morning person. "See Me at nine; see Me at ten" — that would be easy. But at five in the morning, I'm usually sound asleep. Yet this was God issuing an invitation, and I had to respond.

The first ten days were tough. They were like two-a-days at training camp in July or August.[3] I set the alarm, pushed myself out of bed when it rang, and found my way to a quiet spot in the house. Although I was excited about the new venture, it was rough.

Days eleven through fifteen were better, but I still was grinding it out. And then, about day sixteen, things began to click. I found myself praying, "God, I want You to be in me and on me." I didn't know where that prayer came from; it just rose up within me. Later that week I found a verse in the gospel of John that said,

> And I will ask the Father, and he will give you another Coun-
> selor to be with you forever — the Spirit of truth. The world

cannot accept him, because it neither sees him nor knows him. But you know him, for he lives *with you and will be in you.* (14:16–17)

Jesus was asking His Father to send us a Gift, and none of us could have imagined a bigger, more life-changing gift. Jesus sent us the Holy Spirit, who will live "with you and will be in you." I began to get excited, not just about the idea of the Holy Spirit living in me and on me, but by the fact that a prayer, consistent with what Jesus had already said, had come from deep within my spirit. The reference in the gospel of John, "with you and…in you," isn't an exact match to the words I had been praying, but it was very close. "With you and in you; in me and on me." After I saw that verse, getting up early in the morning to spend time with God wasn't such a chore.

As God and I continued our morning visits, He began to break that concept down for me. "In you"—the knowing, inner sense of the presence of the Holy Spirit that says, "Go this way; say these words." The Holy Spirit living inside us guides our life and affects what we do and say on the outside.

"On you"—the miraculous, powerful presence of God made obvious and tangible to others through signs and wonders. As we follow Christ and learn to obey Him, God works in us and uses us in the lives of other people.

During the next few days alone with God, I came to a fresh realization that Jesus really lived and walked on earth. He actually died on the cross, rose again, and sent the Holy Spirit to us. In the process my prayer life took on new energy and importance. When I prayed, the same Spirit whom Jesus sent to His followers was in me and on me. To say I felt a tingling sensation all over sounds a little over the top, but that's the best way

I can describe how I felt. Every cell in my body seemed alive and awake, an experience I'd never had before. My spirit was quickened to the freshness of Scripture.

That new sense of being alive in Christ wasn't confined only to my prayer time early in the mornings. When I prayed for others in meetings or in private, I began to "know" things and "see" things about them. I would picture the person I was praying for, and I'd see some great things and sometimes awful things. At times I would see some very intimate things about the person, but always it would be an insight into what that person needed at the moment. God was giving me these insights, and I was compelled to act. One moment it would be a word or scripture that seemed appropriate and fitting. The next it would be something that had just happened to the person I was praying for, something I had no way of knowing about. And at times it would be something so obvious that it sounded trite. But regardless of how it sounded to me, I did my best to obey God and deliver His message to the person.

At a meeting one night a woman asked me to pray for her. As I touched her hands, I knew in my heart I was supposed to tell her, "Jesus loves you." That sounds like such a cliché, you could easily say, "Very profound, Shaun. The Holy Spirit had to tell you that? Everybody knows Jesus loves us."

Yet I knew in my heart the issue wasn't about theology or slogans or how perceptive it made me appear. The issue was whether I would say those words at that moment to that woman. Would I obey the leading of the Holy Spirit—that still, small voice speaking to me inside—and trust that God knew what He was doing?

It seemed a little awkward, but I smiled at her and said, "You know, I think I'm supposed to tell you, 'Jesus loves you.'" As I said those words, tears came rolling down her cheeks, and she received a tremendous release of the Lord's presence in her life. I don't know anything else about her, and I said nothing else to her that night. But God knew exactly what she needed. For her, hearing those words opened a door inside that allowed God to minister to her. That's the presence of the Holy Spirit in you and on you.

Another time, my cousin Ben had some friends over. I told them about the prayer time I'd been having and about how real God's presence was, not only during morning prayer time, but throughout the day. Later in the evening Ben and his friends and I gathered and began to pray. As we did that, I felt led to go around the group and pray for each person individually.

The first one I prayed for was a guy named Cory. Then I moved to Ben. After him I came to a guy I had never met before that night. As I started to pray, I felt certain I should touch his eyes. When I touched him, I knew the Holy Spirit wanted me to tell him, "You will sleep again." I knew nothing about him, and I had no idea what those words meant, but I said them just the same. I admit that was strange, but I went on praying for his life and future.

When I finished praying for each person, I asked Cory to stand up. I laid my hand on the top of his head and prayed for God to touch him from the top of his head to the soles of his feet. Cory smiled and sat back down. We laughed a little about it, and then I asked Cory what he felt. He said, "Honestly, I didn't know what I was supposed to feel. But when you touched my head and started praying for me, my feet felt like they were on fire."

Afterward, as everyone was leaving, the young man in his early twenties whom I'd never met before that night—the one I had told, "You will sleep again"—took me aside and said, "You were right-on with that prayer about sleep. I haven't been able to sleep much in weeks."

THE SPIRIT IN YOU AND ON YOU

When I was a young boy, I saw a movie called *The Last Dragon*.[4] You probably can still find it in a rental store or on the discount shelf at a big-box retailer. The star of the movie was Leroy Green, a man who never fully believed in himself as a kung fu master. But one day he had to defend the love of his life against a man named Sho'nuf. One of the catch lines from the movie is "Who's the master?" As they fought, Sho'nuf kept asking Leroy, "Who's the master?" With Leroy backed into a corner, Sho'nuf moved in to deliver the knockout punch. As he did, he asked again, "Who's the master?" At that moment Leroy reached up and caught Sho'nuf's fist. Holding it there a moment, he replied, "I am." And with that a glow came over him. He began to kick and punch with more power. He won the fight and the love of the girl. He became the master that was always inside him. It took his being involved in that fight for him to find it.

The Last Dragon is fiction, but there's truth in its message. God offers each of us an anointing in Christ. That anointing is available to every Believer once we find out who we really are in Christ.

My early morning prayer regimen continued for about sixty days. Each day I awakened at five and spent at least an hour with God. During that time the Holy Spirit brought to mind the ideas about God's order that had occurred to me when I read *The Call*. I realized that my new experiences with the power and majesty of God's presence in me and on me had to do with the order God follows when He works in our lives. I marveled at how God had begun a conversation with me two years earlier, then had come back to finish it as if the conversation had never been interrupted.

I heard the Holy Spirit say, "This is what happens when you walk the

Walk. Not perfection. I'm not looking for perfection. I'm looking for order."

In the following chapters we will explore that order—the order of life, the stages through which we grow on the way to spiritual maturity in Christ. God can and does use anyone for anything at any time. But in the broader sense of where He begins with us and where He is taking each of us, there is a divinely appointed order, and there is a progression to the way He works in our lives. God meets us when we are Unbelievers. He speaks to us and reveals Himself, and we become Believers. As we grow in Christ, we become Examples, and then Teachers. And in the lives of many of Christ's followers, God calls them to do the work of Imparters. They do the miraculous work of Christ on earth, just as the first disciples did.

The five stages and their sequence are important: Unbeliever, Believer, Example, Teacher, Imparter. Skip a stage in the maturity process, and error will creep in. Get ahead of God, and things will start to go wrong. But follow His order in your life, and you will see amazing things happen.

PART 1

The Unbeliever

For a Wanderer or a Wonderer,
There Is an Answer

I'm just going with the flow. Whatever
happens, happens.

—THE WANDERER

Is that right? Is that real? How do you know?

—THE WONDERER

CHAPTER 2

A Wanderer and a Wonderer

> For since the creation of the world God's invisible qualities—his eternal power and divine nature—have been clearly seen, being understood from what has been made, so that men are without excuse.
>
> —PAUL, THE APOSTLE (ROMANS 1:20)

When I was a child, my mother took my brother, our friends, and me to church almost every Sunday. At home she lived the life of a Believer in front of us. She loved people and tried to help those in need. I heard biblical preaching at church, and those words went deep into my heart. Yet, despite growing up in an atmosphere of faith, there came a time when I had to say yes to God for myself. That was a defining moment in my life. Beginning with the moment I said yes, God changed my life. I had thought and believed one way before that, and then God began making me into a different person.

God does not withhold His blessings from those who don't yet know Him. The apostle Paul said that God's creation—the beauty of the world around us—shows us God's greatness (see Romans 1:20). Jesus said that God sends His rain to water the fields of both the righteous and the unrighteous (see Matthew 5:45). Before we come to know Him, God is already working in our lives. We all begin life as an Unbeliever.

As Unbelievers, we fall into one of two categories. We are either Wanderers or Wonderers. A Wanderer drifts from place to place, idea to idea. To borrow from Paul, a Wanderer is "tossed back and forth by the waves, and blown here and there by every wind of teaching and by the cunning and craftiness of men in their deceitful scheming" (Ephesians 4:14). Wanderers are interested in ideas and various beliefs. They flow with something, and at times with *anything,* that can direct their lives.

On the other hand, Wonderers approach life with a sense of purpose. They are searching for something that will reveal life's deeper meaning. Wonderers know already that they have a greater purpose. They are painfully aware that something is not complete. The hollowness of post-modern life is ever-present, and though they crave relief from that uncertainty, they don't know where to turn.

THE WANDERER

When I think of a Wanderer, I think of dandelions that have gone to seed. The bloom grows at the end of a green stem, and when the flower dries and forms seeds, the top looks like a white fuzzball. When you blow on it, the seed particles scatter like pieces of lint. When I was a kid, we used to pick them, hold them up to our lips, and blow. The fuzz flew from the stem, then drifted quietly across the yard and into oblivion. As the seeds disappeared from view, I imagined where they would go. They might land somewhere in our yard or in the neighbor's garden or in a flower bed where they could sprout and grow. But no matter where they landed, I knew they had no control over where they were going. They were blown along by the wind, drifting on currents of air that could take them anywhere.

Wanderers are like that. They're blown along by whatever comes their way. When I meet a wandering Unbeliever, I often think of what he might become if only he could rise above his circumstances to look for meaning and seek the truth.

Often Wanderers don't realize the aimless nature of their life because they have been taught to live that way. They are subject to their environment. Like dandelions gone to seed, they have no control over the direction they take.

Wanderers give little thought to what they are doing and the result it will produce. Many of them have heard of Jesus and have tried church. But they regard Jesus and the church as little more than something that is moral and good, and they believe they can take it or leave it. This is no reason to criticize or reject them. God judges people where they are, and so should we. "Since you call on a Father who judges each man's work impartially, live your lives as strangers here in reverent fear" (1 Peter 1:17; see also Romans 2:14–15). God judges all. So don't judge the Wanderers; love them.

Many Believers started out as Wanderers, and then their lives began to change when someone took an interest in them. To have a positive impact on them, you have to love them into God's Kingdom. That is how Jesus seeks them, with grace and mercy.

Scripture says our enemy roars "like a…lion looking for someone to devour" (1 Peter 5:8). Satan is out looking for Wanderers since they are easy targets. He searches for the wounded, the hurting, those who are not alert to the danger. When you're a Wanderer, you never feel like you're under attack, and you don't realize you are vulnerable to deception. Satan tells you a lie that seems harmless. You become convinced that you are doing fine on your own, and you're sure there is no truth that is worthy of your trust. You believe there are no reliable answers to your questions. You take one step closer, not realizing you've triggered a trap until you feel the jaws of that trap sinking into your flesh.

As you wade deeper into the lies, you still don't realize it's a trap. You indulge in a lingering look at pornography, venture further into sexual experimentation, go along with alcohol or a fling with drugs. They all seem harmless. Then you find that doing these things has touched a much deeper area of your life, tapping into hidden tendencies and releasing appetites you can't control. The next thing you know, a vice has you in its grip, and you're not sure you'll ever break free. Later in life you realize you are trapped in strongholds that began with choices you made while you were yet an Unbeliever. This is where these things begin.

THE WONDERER

Wonderers are Unbelievers who have a lot of questions but no answers. They wonder about the meaning of life. Is there any purpose to it, or is life only what we make of it? Restless and unsettled, they have no foundational beliefs to hold on to except the ones they make for themselves.

When I think of a Wonderer, I think of a kid I once saw who was mad at the world. He knew something had gone terribly wrong, but he didn't know what to do to make things right. Instead, he would punch and kick at the air. He wasn't shadowboxing, the way a boxer will practice moves by punching at an imaginary opponent. This kid was just punching and kicking the air for no purpose other than to vent his anger and frustration. He wasn't perfecting a skill; he was simply fighting the air and doing nothing to find answers to his questions.

Wonderers have a sense that life holds more than what they're experiencing. They say things like, "There has to be more to life. There must be something out there that would make me more satisfied." Or they might say, "I need to find something to do or somebody to help, a cause to invest myself in. I'm missing something."

Whether things are going bad, good, or just okay, Wonderers know they are seeking something more. They just don't know what it is. In their hearts they sense that life must have more to offer, but they don't know how to find it. Locked in a vicious cycle, they try all kinds of projects and activities, but nothing they attempt answers their questions or changes their circumstances.

I once saw two young girls tossing a ball back and forth. They stood a few feet apart and were having fun for a while. Then one of them wanted more. She didn't know what, exactly. She just wanted something more—a game with meaning. I heard her tell the other girl, "Let's play a new game. Whoever catches the ball the tenth time loses." The little girl who spoke went first. They tossed the ball back and forth, counting each time. The ball went from one girl to the other, and on the tenth toss landed in the hands of the girl who had started the game.

"Oh," she giggled. "I lost. Let's play again."

Again they tossed the ball back and forth. And again the ball came back on the tenth toss to the girl who had suggested the new game. This went on, and the little girl grew more and more frustrated. I thought, *How does she not know that if she tosses the ball first, she will always begin the game on an odd number and receive it on an even one?* She would always lose at this game. Finally she gave up and suggested they play something else.

That game gives us a good image of the Wonderer. She may be happy or sad, nice or mean, good or bad, but it makes no difference. Whatever she does, she still gets the same result. She knows something is not complete, and she wants more out of the game, but she has no answers.

Wonderers often are people who were raised in the church. They know the religious words to use and can give you all the clichéd answers. Some of them, even while continuing to attend on Sundays, are jaded about their church experience. They have been burned by an institution that too often concentrates on numbers and programs rather than individuals and lives. I've met many children of preachers who wonder what it would be like to go wild, to be free to chase the pleasures of the world. They wonder what that world is like and whether the things their parents teach is the truth.

Some Wonderers are a lot like an NFL quarterback I know. He was a franchise player, someone with outstanding ability who could lead a championship team. During this man's career, his team won many games, including league championships and even the Super Bowl. But later, when he was asked about playing and winning and how it related to his life, he replied, "If earning a lot of money and winning the Super Bowl is all there is in life, I'm in trouble. Because I've done that, and there's still something missing." I've heard those words from him and many others.

That's a Wonderer. He knows enough to realize that the life he is living can't be all there is, but he doesn't know what the real answer is. Wonderers know they have a longing inside for something, but they can't identify what's missing. Like a person stumbling around in a dark room, their only hope is to one day stumble upon the light.

Meanwhile they wonder about life.

"Why am I here?"

"What am I doing with my life?"

"Why do things go that way?"

"Does anyone ask the same questions I do?"

GOD REACHES A WONDERER

One autumn Sunday after church, a woman I'd never seen before came up to me. In her eyes I saw something very good and something that seemed very wrong. She said, "My son really needs to talk to you." She pointed him out, a teenager named Aaron, in a crowd at the back of the church.

I walked back there and introduced myself. I told him, "Meet me here for the youth service on Wednesday night. We can talk then." He assured me he'd be there.

In a normal year I would have been playing football on that Sunday morning. That year, however, was the year the Seahawks cut me from the team. Because I had my Sundays free, I was present when Aaron and his mother came to church.

The following Wednesday I arrived at church and saw Aaron sitting with some other high school kids. After the service we talked, but it was very low-key. As I left that evening, I said, "I'll see you on Sunday. Sit next to me."

Aaron was there the following Sunday, and we sat together. We talked and joked around, but that was as far as the conversation went. After the service I suggested he attend the youth service again on Wednesday night. He returned that week, and after the service I drove him home. As we rode toward his house, I said, "Tell me your story."

"Okay," Aaron said and opened right up.

Near the end of the previous summer, a girl in his neighborhood came to him and said, "I'm going to give you an early birthday present." As you might guess, that present was sexual intercourse. It was Aaron's first sexual experience. Between the time of that experience and the beginning of school, Aaron had sex with a number of girls. With his senses suddenly alive, he indulged in other forms of stimulation. He started drinking alcohol and then moved to marijuana. From there he went on to a drug known as Ecstasy.

Ecstasy comes in pill form and is available just about everywhere teenagers get together. It's a form of methamphetamine that can produce a heightened sense of pleasure or increased alertness. It also can kill you. Much of what is sold on the street as Ecstasy is contaminated with all kinds of substances. No one really knows how his body will react to this drug until *after* he swallows it.

Aaron, as I learned, never got into anything slowly. He would go all out from the beginning, and he was into Ecstasy in a big way. One night at a party he took an Ecstasy pill. A few minutes later he took another. Still not satisfied, he wanted to take a third but was afraid of what might happen. So he cut a pill in half. Even at that, his friends told him that was risky and that he could die.

Aaron was scared. All night he worried that he had crossed a line from which he might never return. As he worried about dying, he became convinced he needed to change the way he was living. A day or two later he told his mother he wanted to go to church. She wasn't attending church at the time, but our church was just down the street from where they lived. The Sunday she approached me about talking to Aaron was their first Sunday there.

When we reached Aaron's house that Wednesday night, he and I sat in the car and talked some more. I opened my Bible and shared a few verses with him about temptation and how God provides a way out. I told him how Jesus was tempted in the same ways we are and that being tempted wasn't bad. We just had to learn how to react to it. I talked to Aaron about salvation and the Believer's walk with God.

And then I did something very strange. I said, "I think I'm supposed to touch your nose."

He said, "Okay."

I know it sounds strange, but I had this overwhelming sense that I was supposed to do that, so I gently laid the palm of my hand along the tip of his nose. He took a breath, and his eyes opened wide. "Oh, wow," he exclaimed. "I can't believe it." From the look on his face, I could see he was getting a rush.

Aaron was a kid who experienced life through his senses. He would have been sensory oriented whether he used Ecstasy or not. That he had used drugs did not prevent God from meeting him right where he was.

Sex and drugs had offered him apparent pleasure, but they had become a trap. Aaron needed Someone to set him free from that trap. That's exactly what God did for him.

I took my hand off the tip of his nose, and Aaron looked down and took a deep breath. He looked up at me with a smile and said, "That was better than Ecstasy!"

I laughed and said, "Yes, He is. Yes, God is. God sure is."

A month later I signed with the Washington Redskins and moved to northern Virginia. After the season ended, I caught up with Aaron.

"How's it going?"

"Great," he replied.

I joked, "How's the E world?"

"I'm a legend," he laughed. "I'm the only kid around who quit Ecstasy cold turkey and never had any side effects. And I never wanted to go back to it, either."

From that day, Aaron got involved in a discipleship group and has never taken Ecstasy again.

THE WHAT AND THE WHY OF LIFE

Every night before our children go to bed, I go up to their room and have a question-and-answer session with them before we pray. When I was a young boy, my mother used to talk with us every night in much the same way. She would ask about our day, and we'd discuss the things that had happened. Doing that helped me think about the what and why of my life, and it helped me focus my prayers. I do the same with my children as we wrap up the day and get ready for the next.

One night, when our oldest daughters were four and five, I went up to their room for the nightly session. The day had been stressful. Both of them had been through reprimands, time-outs, and every possible form of acceptable discipline, and still they had trouble behaving. So as we were winding down for the night, my oldest girl asked if good people go to heaven and bad people go to hell. The question was surprising, but I knew it had come from the kind of day we'd had. It afforded me a great opportunity to be a father and a Teacher. In reply I said, "Being good doesn't get you to heaven, and being bad doesn't get you to hell."

She asked, "Then how do you get to heaven?"

I explained to her that being good or bad wasn't the point. We get to heaven by loving Jesus.

Wanderers and Wonderers are like our children, just looking for something to believe in. Some have questions; some don't. Our role as Believers is to love them up to the level of asking questions and then love them into the answers.

CHAPTER 3

Trials, Traps, and Victories

For the Son of Man came to seek
and to save what was lost.
—JESUS OF NAZARETH (LUKE 19:10)

Every step on the path to spiritual maturity is accompanied by a trial, a trap, and a victory. Enduring the trial, avoiding the trap, and obtaining the victory are the keys to spiritual survival and the path to moving on to the next stage of spiritual maturity.

In this life everything is learned: the way we act, the way we think, the way we view the world around us. Salvation brings instant justification before God, but it doesn't undo all the things that are not right with us. The process through which we are renewed, the means by which our thoughts, actions, and character are transformed, comes through learned lessons—what the Bible calls trials. Those trying experiences show us what we're made of, reveal what's inside us, and expose what really matters most. When handled correctly, they open doors of learning and growth that not only impart information but also reach to the depths of our motivations and bring lasting change.

The trials we encounter come from different directions, but God uses them all to instill His character qualities in us. Scripture refers to those qualities as the fruit of the Spirit. "The fruit of the Spirit is love, joy, peace, patience, kindness, goodness, faithfulness, gentleness and self control" (Galatians 5:22–23). The fruit of the Spirit is a description of God's character. When Scripture refers to God's unchanging nature, it is referring to these nine traits. God's character restrains His power and focuses that power in a particular direction. He does not act on a whim or impulse. He always acts in a manner consistent with His character, which guides Him in the use of His power.[1]

To instill His character in us, God has to subject us to teachable moments. Scripture calls those moments "suffering." This is why Paul says, "Suffering produces perseverance; perseverance, character; and character, hope. And hope does not disappoint us" (Romans 5:3–5).

When I think of suffering and trials, I think of attending summer camps when I was playing PeeWee League football or participating in the summer practices at the University of Alabama or training camp in the NFL. During those camps we worked out twice each day, running the same drills over and over again. Each drill was designed to teach our muscles a new way of acting and to do it without our having to think about it. It took repeated drills to break a bad habit and instill a good one. Two-a-days in the hot August sun are the trials of a football player.

Unbelievers have trials as well. God uses those trials for the same purpose: to instill His character qualities in an Unbeliever. Because an Unbeliever doesn't yet believe, God's immediate purpose is to move him to a place where it will be easier to believe. God uses the circumstances of the Unbeliever's life to push him toward that moment, but because of the Unbeliever's condition, he is much more vulnerable to the traps.

THE TRIALS OF THE WANDERER

The trial for a Wanderer, one who is not asking about the hows and whys of life, is to survive the dangers of life long enough to get to ask those questions. An individual who sees no need to ask questions about life, who sees no purpose in life beyond enduring each day, fails to sense the threats. If you think I'm imagining things, visit a local jail and talk to some of the inmates. You'll hear many of them say they have no idea how they got involved in the activities that led to their incarceration. They can tell you about the incident that got them arrested. They just can't tell you why it happened to them or how their life prior to that could have turned out differently. The fact that some of them made choices that led to their arrest is beyond their comprehension. To them, it "just happened." Worse still, they don't understand that other people live in a very different way.

If Wanderers survive long enough to start considering the questions of life, they might make it. But for now, they are trapped in a lie, and they don't know it. They've been told that lie by Satan for the purpose of keeping them ignorant of the truth. The truth they need to hear is that they are slaves to the randomness of events around them, slaves to sin, slaves to the iniquity of generations before them. The key to the Wanderer's growth is reaching a point where he is no longer satisfied with life as it is. Wanderers need to finally ask the real questions and press on to find real answers.

THE TRIALS OF THE WONDERER

The challenge for Wonderers, those who ask the essential questions of life but have no answers, is much the same as for Wanderers. They must endure long enough to find the Spirit of Truth. However, Wonderers begin in a somewhat better place. They already sense there is more to life than merely existing from one day to the next, and they have a sense of destiny. They just don't know what that destiny might be or how they might find it.

Jesus gave us the answer to our longings when He said, "The Counselor, the Holy Spirit, whom the Father will send in my name, will teach you all things and will remind you of everything I have said to you" (John 14:26). The Holy Spirit leads us into all truth—truth about Scripture, about life, about who we are and the identity God has made for us. He begins that work by leading us to salvation in Christ, which we receive after our open and conscious acknowledgment that Jesus is Savior and Lord.

At their core, the Wonderer's questions about meaning and purpose are the same questions we all ask God: Why does this happen? What does this mean? Wonderers also want to know what and who is out there: Who are You? Who do You see when You look at me? Can I make it? Do I have the "stuff"? Wonderers spend a lot of time thinking about these things; they just don't know they are asking God these questions.

Many Wonderers are sitting in the pews of our churches. They know the language of religion, but they don't know God and have not yielded to His work in their lives. Knowing the language of religion can be dangerous, because it seduces Wonderers into thinking they have already had the experience of finding God. Like a flu shot, it gives them a small dose that prevents them from receiving the real thing. In that sense their knowledge of a few religious or theological concepts insulates them from a genuine relationship with God.

Breaking through this deception can be a tough task, and it's not one that can be accomplished by reason alone. Like the boy who used to punch and kick the air, the Wonderer swings aimlessly at questions, hoping for answers, but often lacks the patience to receive them.

THE TRAPS OF THE UNBELIEVER

For the Unbeliever, there is always a trap. Football teams have a play called a trap. In a basic trap play, an offensive lineman blocks the defensive player who is positioned to his left or right, leaving the player directly in front of him free to cross the line of scrimmage. To the unsuspecting defensive lineman, it looks like an easy opportunity to tackle the running back behind the line for a loss of yardage. Looks, however, can be deceiving. While the defender is focused on tackling the running back, an offensive lineman comes running from the opposite side of the line. The defender doesn't see him until it's too late. The trapped defender gets hit from the side by a lineman moving at full speed. The force of that impact knocks the defender out of the way just as the running back approaches with the ball. The running back accelerates through the hole and pops into the defensive backfield, avoiding the three-hundred-pound men on the defensive line and having to contend with linebackers, safeties, or cornerbacks.

That's a trap play in football. Properly executed, it opens up before the other team realizes what's happening, and it closes on the unsuspecting player before he can react. It works so well because the defensive lineman follows an almost irresistible impulse to pick up an easy tackle. Spiritual traps are a lot like that. Often we walk into them totally unaware, only to be hit from the blind side.

My brother and I were latchkey kids. Our mother worked, so she was not at home when we arrived from school. We had a key and let ourselves into the apartment, but no one was there to supervise us. We usually did what was right and stayed out of trouble, but we were boys, and trouble can find boys long before they go looking for it.

One day, hours before our mother came home from work, a number of us gathered at a friend's house. We all were latchkey kids. The boy who was hosting the unsupervised group took us into his parents' bedroom and showed us his father's collection of pornographic magazines. They were laid out on the bed, open and easy to see. I glanced at one, then another, and then left the room. But a quick look at the pictures was all it took.

In that unguarded, unprotected moment, my sense of sexuality was set on fire. The hormones in my adolescent body were like gasoline, and the magazines were like a torch. When I walked in that house, I had no intention of looking at those kinds of magazines. When I entered the bedroom, I didn't know what everyone else was looking at, but I looked. And I looked a little too long.

The temptation to view pornography was like a seed that would land whenever I allowed a small opening for it. Many others have struggled in greater ways, and some of the stories I've heard are way crazier than mine. The battle to break free from pornography can consume a person's life far more extensively than what I experienced. But we've all fallen into the same trap, one that took me more than a decade to get out of. All traps have the goal to take you out, and it's easy to get stuck in one without intending to.

Like the trap play in football, the trap for a Wanderer and a Wonderer springs before the person knows it. Drugs, alcohol, and improper sexual activity don't come with a sign that says, "Try me once, and I will destroy your life." Marijuana, cocaine, or any other drug doesn't come with pictures of the physical damage and ruined relationships that the drugs produce. One night of hookup sex doesn't have a picture attached to it that shows the deadly effects of AIDS. The trap presents the promise of pleasure and excitement and stirs your longing for love. But the only thing that is delivered is a counterfeit of love, and even a counterfeit of fun. By then you are engaged in the deception, and you're in the grip of the trap.

Human nature has been corrupted by sin, but by God's grace and mercy, He has forgiven us in Jesus. We can find in Him the wisdom and strength to say no and to resist giving in to the flesh and its desires. God's grace gives us the ability to respond like Jesus, to stand strong against temptation (see 1 Corinthians 10:13). However, as humans, our ability to follow Christ has limits. Believers have the Holy Spirit living inside them, so they have God's power to help them live an obedient life. But Unbelievers—both Wanderers and Wonderers—run the risk of having little or no wherewithal to resist temptation, to escape the trap, and to seek God. If they resist God's overtures, ignore the twinge of conscience, and seek instead their own pleasure or the latest spiritual fad, they risk moving beyond a tipping point from which they cannot return. Scripture describes this in Paul's letter to the Romans: "They exchanged the truth of God for a lie, and worshiped and served created things rather than the Creator.... Because of this, God gave them over to shameful lusts" (Romans 1:25–26).

In his book *Surprised by Joy,* C. S. Lewis describes an incident that illustrates the trap an Unbeliever faces. Lewis grew up in the Anglican Church and had a basic understanding of God. He knew the correct religious language. As a young man, he attended a boarding school. The school's matron was into the occult, and she, somewhat unwittingly, exposed Lewis to occult practices and ideas.

> Now it so happened that Miss C., who seemed old to me, was still in her spiritual immaturity, was still hunting, with the eagerness of a soul that had a touch of angelic quality in it, for a truth and a way of life. Guides were even rarer then than now. She was (as I should now put it) floundering in the mazes of Theosophy, Rosicrucianism, Spiritualism; the whole Anglo-American Occultist tradition.[2]

Those ideas and practices found in Lewis a ready welcome, and they exploded in his mind and in his heart.

> And that started in me something with which, on and off, I have had plenty of trouble since—the desire for the preternatural, simply as such, the passion for the Occult. Not everyone has this

disease; those who have will know what I mean. I once tried to describe it in a novel. It is a spiritual lust; and like the lust of the body it has the fatal power of making everything else in the world seem disinteresting while it lasts.[3]

Lewis was not searching for the occult; it came to him at an early age and inflamed in him a desire for those practices and beliefs. Once the ideas produced an emotional response within him, everything else was of no interest. He could not easily free himself from the clutches of either the passion or the ideas. Although he later renounced the ideas, he continued to struggle with an emotional inclination toward occult beliefs for the remainder of his life.

The Wanderer and the Wonderer are both adrift on a sea of ideas and open to whatever they encounter—the former to whatever happens in his life, the latter to whatever he can dream up. The things in life that excite our senses and produce great physical stimulation, such as sex, drugs, and alcohol, carry with them the trap of great pain. It is easy for Satan to use those things to deceive the unwary person.

Earlier we discussed God's work in our lives, that He follows a certain order. He established that order for our protection, to keep each aspect of life in its proper place. Take things in God's order, and blessings will follow. Take things out of order, and trouble erupts. In the context God intended and in the right order, those things bring intense pleasure and complement every other aspect of our lives. But get them out of order, and something that was supposed to be a blessing becomes a beast.

THE VICTORIES OF THE UNBELIEVER

God's desire for both Wanderers and Wonderers is that they become Believers. At first, of course, when Unbelievers commit their lives to Christ, they are not mature Believers. They are not sure how it all fits together, but they believe. That is the victory. Not in immediately righting all the wrongs in their lives or undoing the destructive habits that formed around the traps that ensnared them. Initially, taking the step from Unbeliever to Believer involves merely believing. Scripture sums up saving faith this way: "If you confess with your mouth, 'Jesus is Lord,' and believe in your heart that God raised him from the dead, you will be saved" (Romans 10:9).

That passage gives us two steps to salvation: believe in your heart, and confess with your mouth.

Although Jesus cautioned His disciples against swearing oaths, the act of confessing is very different. As Scripture uses the term in Romans, confessing is very much like making a vow of loyalty. Today we have become jaded in our view of a person's assurances that he or she is telling the truth. The old saying "The check's in the mail" arose from that skepticism. A person's word doesn't mean much anymore. But in history, oaths were not made lightly. Ancient society looked on them as sacred. If the information given under the assurance of an oath turned out to be knowingly false, the one making the false statement might pay for it with his life. That is what Scripture means when it says "confess with your mouth."

In English literature, the heart is often used to mean the seat of one's emotions or will. "He broke her heart" means he caused her great anguish in the form of emotional pain. When we say, "That boy has a lot of heart," we mean he has a firm resolve to see some task or endeavor through to the end, no matter what. When Paul used the term *heart* in the passage from Romans, he didn't mean only the seat of human will and emotions. He was referring to the core of human self-consciousness, which includes both intellect and spirit. Believing with one's heart means that nothing is held in reserve. Everything is on the line and at risk.

The two together, confessing specifically that Jesus is Lord and believing with your heart that God raised Him from the dead, open the door to salvation.

This is the point Paul reached on the road to Damascus. He had believed in God most of his life. He just didn't believe that Jesus was the Christ—the Messiah. And he certainly didn't believe that Jesus had died and been raised again. Following the crucifixion, Paul set out to rid the world of Christians. He kicked down doors and dragged believers into the streets. He would haul them before the Sanhedrin on charges of heresy. He watched as they were beaten, whipped, and sometimes stoned to death.

After rampaging through Jerusalem, Paul obtained letters from the Sanhedrin authorizing him to do the same in Damascus. He was on his way there to continue the persecution when Jesus appeared to him. As a result of that encounter, two things happened. Paul was struck blind, and he became a Believer. He moved from the kingdom of darkness to the kingdom of light with one simple response.

"'Who are you, Lord?' Saul [Paul] asked.

"'I am Jesus, whom you are persecuting,' he [Christ] replied" (Acts 9:5).

At the time Paul did not understand all the theological implications of Jesus' resurrection. That would come later. But he knew that Jesus was alive. This was the most important moment of his life: he realized that Jesus, the Son of God, had died and then risen from the dead. Yet Paul's response was not complicated or encumbered with religious language. He didn't recite a prayer from a religious tract or respond to an altar call at church. He simply asked that one question, "Who are you, Lord?" With those few words, his conversion was complete, a fact to which God bore witness. "This man is my chosen instrument to carry my name before the Gentiles and their kings and before the people of Israel. I will show him how much he must suffer for my name" (Acts 9:15–16).

Although Paul's understanding was incomplete, that single experience on the way to Damascus changed the direction of his life and the direction of Western civilization. It all began with a moment. For the Wanderer and the Wonderer, believing is just that simple and just that dynamic.

CHAPTER 4

Peter Walks into Real Belief

Just because you're talking to Jesus
doesn't make you a Believer.
—SHAUN ALEXANDER

Most of the New Testament was written originally in Greek. Unlike English, Greek has more than one word for time: *kronos* and *kairos.*

The word *kronos* denotes time as a sequence or succession of moments. This is where we get the English word *chronology* and our chronological understanding of time. *Kairos* in ancient Greek also refers to time. That sense of time goes beyond the mere tracking of minutes or hours or days. Instead, it describes the quality of the moment. A kairos moment is a moment that brings with it some particular quality. It is what we often refer to as a defining moment. For the Unbeliever a kairos moment presents a choice, either to believe or not to believe. In that moment the choice is to surrender in faith to Jesus or not to.

The first kairos moment is described in the gospel of John: "In the beginning was the Word, and the Word was with God, and the Word was God. He was with God in the beginning. Through him all things were made; without him nothing was made that has been made" (John 1:1–3). Jesus, the Word, was present at the creation of the world. He was there when the sun and moon were put in place, and He was there when Adam and Eve were formed. In fact, He was the means by which all of creation came into being (see Colossians 1:15–17). When the disciples walked with Jesus through Galilee, they were walking with the One who created all that exists. It took some time before they realized who He was and who they were because of Him. That moment of belief became their kairos moment, a moment that defined them as Believers.

The summer before I entered the seventh grade, one of my PeeWee football teammates invited several of us over to his house. We played football in the park down the street and then walked to the store for a snack. At that age, going to the store on our own was a big deal.

While we were there, I saw one of my teammates put a candy bar in his pocket. I said, "What are you doing?"

"Nobody ever sees us when we do it," he replied. "Take one."

At the sound of those words, everything seemed to move in slow motion. I grabbed his arm and said, "I can't do it. If we get caught, I'd get in trouble."

We walked out of the store with only the things we had purchased, but for me it was a kairos moment, a moment that defined who I really was. That moment is still burned in my memory because it marked me as a person who lived by a moral standard. Ever since that moment, I have made many choices in life based on that experience.

A kairos moment marks you for life, often setting a new course that points you to God. It also can work in the opposite direction, turning you away from God or directing you into a period of searching and experimentation.

Robert, a young man I mentored, was a genuine man of God from a young age. All through high school he lived by a standard of purity and godliness. He didn't drink alcohol, never used drugs, didn't use profanity, and avoided sex. Then, during his freshmen year in college, he met a young woman, and they began to date. She was a Christian, and they made themselves accountable for their relationship and how they expressed affection for each other. For three years they conducted themselves as a couple who loved Jesus.

During the summer before their senior year, however, their relationship began to turn. They started to drift apart, and Robert feared the relationship was slipping away. Feeling desperate, he decided to do whatever it took to hold on to his girlfriend. Within a matter of weeks, they had sex together. That was a kairos moment in Robert's life. It marked him as a person who gave up his commitment to obey God's requirements regarding sex in order to get something he desired. The catch is, he lost the relationship anyway.

If you talk to Robert today, he'll tell you that stepping out of God's order for his life was a monumental mistake, one of the worst things he ever did. It never works, no matter what it is you want. For Robert, the kairos moment of choosing to have sex to try to hold on to his girlfriend worked in the opposite direction. It defined for him the person he was not.

A MAN REBUKED, THEN HONORED

Peter, a man whom Jesus both rebuked ("Get behind me, Satan!") and honored ("on this rock I will build my church") was familiar with kairos moments (see Mark 8:33 and Matthew 16:18). His life was shaped by these moments in dramatic and even world-changing ways.

When Jesus found him, Peter was earning his living as a fisherman in Capernaum, a town on the northern shore of the Sea of Galilee. The town sat in a region of Israel that was influenced by both Greco-Roman and radical Jewish thought. The winds of change were blowing, and many Jews were expecting the Messiah to appear at any moment. Peter was among those who were searching for the Christ. He knew the Messiah would come and bring change, but Peter had no idea what the Messiah would look like, how He would act, or what it would mean for his own life.

At the time some thought the Messiah would come as a mighty warrior and vanquish the Romans, who were occupying Judea. Others thought He would come as a king and establish again the kingdom of Israel as it had been in the golden age of David. Radicals of every kind traveled the region, teaching in synagogues, private homes, and public forums. Many of them claimed to be the Messiah, and more than one attempted to start a rebellion against the Romans.[1]

Instead of coming as a warrior, a political firebrand, or an earthly king, Jesus came as a humble carpenter. For thirty years He was quiet, loyal, and obedient as He waited for the right moment. And when that moment came, He revealed Himself not to the educated theologians or powerful religious leaders but to a group composed primarily of hardworking, unsophisticated laborers.

The kairos moment when Jesus revealed Himself as the Messiah, when He defined for the world who He really was, became a kairos moment for Peter as well. And when that moment came, Peter did not hesitate to respond.

Scripture says that when Jesus called Peter, he and his brother Andrew "at once...left their nets and followed him" (Mark 1:18). They didn't debate the issue or ask around the community, nor did they call a family gathering to seek everyone's opinion. Jesus called; they got moving. They had been looking for the Messiah for a long time. They had known there must be more to life, but they didn't find it until the day Jesus appeared. In an instant they were changed, and their lives were never the same.

Moments before Jesus found him, Peter was standing in the water, casting his net into the sea as he had done almost every morning of his life. Dressed only in a loincloth, he was hot and sweaty. When he stepped out of the water, answering the call of Jesus, he smelled like fish, and his hands were grimy. But inside, Peter was different.

Peter would toss fishing nets a few more times in his life, and he would push out into the sea in a boat again, but fishing was no longer the source of his identity. The sound of Jesus' voice changed all that. From that day, Peter no longer thought of himself as a fisherman. He no longer saw himself as merely a man of the sea. He was a man of the Christ, a follower of the Way, a disciple of Jesus the Messiah.

That is the victory of the Unbeliever, the victory of the Wanderer and the Wonderer. They aren't perfect, and they don't have a full understanding of God. But they can hear Jesus call them and can reach the point of commitment. Their lifestyle, habits, and personal appearance look the same the moment after they believe as they did the moment before. Yet their sense of identity and the orientation of their lives are completely different.

They believe, and that brings them through the door of salvation.

PART 2

The Believer

Immediately the [sick] boy's father
exclaimed, "I do believe; help me
overcome my unbelief!"

—MARK 9:24

CHAPTER 5

Life as a Believer

Where is your faith?

—JESUS OF NAZARETH (LUKE 8:25)

f you've ever been in church, especially in the South, you've heard
a version of the story about the man who walked a high wire between the Twin Towers of the World Trade Center. Philippe Petit
actually did walk between the two New York City buildings in August
1974.[1] He strung a wire from one building rooftop to the other, and then,
as the morning rush hour began, he started across. Petit was walking
through the air, balanced on amazingly thin footing and eventually danc-
ing on the wire.

New York City always is a busy place, but the busyness of morning
rush hour was no match for a man walking on a narrow wire between the
towers. First one pedestrian and then another stopped to look up as Petit
made his way across, then back. Before the morning was over, the police
arrested him, but by the time his case reached the court, he had become
so popular that the city decided not to prosecute him.

As the story is usually told from a pulpit, Philippe Petit walked from
one building to the other, then came back to the first building. The crowd
was excited and clapped for him. Then Petit asked if anyone thought he
could make the trip across and back while blindfolded. Naturally, hands
went up in a show of support. The crowd was certain Petit could do it.

So he blindfolded himself and walked to the opposite building, then turned and made his way back.

Upon his return he stepped off the wire for a moment and came back with a wheelbarrow. He asked if anyone thought he could make the trip while pushing a wheelbarrow. Of course, an even greater number of people raised their hands, indicating they believed he could succeed in such a trip. Petit then pointed to the nearest person who had raised his hand and asked, "Would you care to ride with me?"

Riding in a wheelbarrow across a wire strung between what were then the tallest buildings in the United States, with someone else in charge of your destiny, is a good metaphor for the life of a Believer. You're going somewhere, but you aren't sure where, and you aren't in control. Risk and danger surround you. You might not make it across safely, but you're going anyway.

None of this would make sense except that you know and trust the One who is pushing the wheelbarrow.

A priest once described the life of a Believer as taking everything you own, pushing it up to the line at a craps table, and handing God the dice. I don't advocate gambling, but you get the picture. Becoming a Believer changes your perspective. You have decided that you are no longer in charge, and you're trusting God with your life and your future.

My oldest brother is in the army. He served in Iraq during the Gulf War. He's now a sergeant and works at a military base in the United States, training soldiers for combat duty. I asked him about war. He told me that most of the soldiers he trains are so committed to the cause that they willingly go into combat, even if it means they will die. That's commitment: going into battle even if you know ahead of time there's a strong possibility you won't come back alive.

LAYING DOWN YOUR LIFE

We all remember the September 11, 2001, attacks on the Twin Towers of
the World Trade Center. Many of the people who died in those buildings
were firefighters, men and women who rushed into the burning buildings
knowing they might never return. Most of the first responders who entered the towers did not survive, yet they went in anyway. That was their
calling. It is also the nature of a Believer's calling. "Whatever You want,
Lord, I'm all-in."

Scripture says, "Now faith is being sure of what we hope for and certain of what we do not see" (Hebrews 11:1). Another translation says,
"Faith is the assurance of things hoped for, the conviction of things not
seen" (RSV).

The faith necessary for salvation is simply the belief that Jesus is
Lord—He is the Christ, the Son of the living God—and that God raised
Him from the dead. His sacrifice on the cross paid the debt for our sins
so that we can stand justified before God. Just as Christ is our Lord, He
also is our Savior. As you grow in your relationship with God, faith becomes a crucial factor in everyday life. It becomes a source of power in
your choices and decisions. But in the beginning, a new Believer has only
that simple belief in Jesus as Lord and Savior. We bring only a *yes* to the
call of God, and that *yes* makes us Believers.

Faith is our agreeing to the truth of what God has already told us.
And although Believers enter into faith by a simple confession of belief,
I know some people who have made that confession numerous times. A
person becomes a Believer with only one confession. Those who make
the same confession over and over usually are facing one of two things.
Either they have habitual sin in their life that they haven't surrendered
to the Holy Spirit, or they are simply hungry for more of God, and their

continued confession is actually a continual prayer to Him for more of His presence in their lives.

Unsurrendered habitual sin

The first issue often results when Unbelievers make a "security blanket" confession. They confess faith in Christ to obtain what appears to be a spiritual insurance policy against the fires of hell, but later they find themselves committing the same sins they struggled with before. The sin crops up in an area of their life that isn't under the control of Christ, often a habit that began early in life. After they commit that sin, they feel guilty about it and pray the "I'm sorry and I'll never do it again" prayer. Or they go to church and respond to the altar call at the end of the service in order to apologize to God.

The problem in either case is that they know in advance that if the opportunity arises again, they will most likely commit the same sin again. This struggle is not evidence of a lack of faith in God but an indication that a spiritual stronghold exists in their life. Merely apologizing won't fix the problem. Making another confession of faith is not a secret formula to rid your life of habitual sin. God doesn't want your apology; He wants your heart. True repentance leads to a changed life, because you are handing over control of your life, choices, words, attitudes, and actions—at every moment—to God.

A hunger for more of God

The second struggle has nothing to do with unsurrendered sin or a stronghold in your life. Instead, it's a matter of hungering for more of God's presence in your life. There are Believers who confess their faith in Christ again and again because they feel they are not experiencing enough of Christ's presence and power. They keep coming to the altar to assure themselves that they are right with God and not blocking His presence. Of course, one confession is all they need to make. One *yes* to Jesus is sufficient for salvation. But one *yes* is not always enough for the things He wants to work on in our lives.

You will continue to face moments of decision as the Holy Spirit moves deeper into your life. At each of the moments, He will ask you to surrender a new level of yourself to Him. My bride, Valerie, came to God this way. She kept coming to Him until she had the inner assurance that she was His and He was hers. At each of those breakthrough points, when you press through to God and yield to Him at a new level, you receive fresh assurance of His presence and a renewed zeal for the work He is doing in and through you.

The moments when you are challenged to go deeper and to allow God to go deeper into your life come in increments. God doesn't immediately throw you into the heat of battle, even though it feels like it sometimes. The first time you have to explain to someone what you believe and why can be a harrowing experience. Those are the experiences that drive you to the Scriptures and drive you to your knees. They force you to decide what you believe and in Whom you believe.

I came to know the Lord on Easter Sunday when I was ten years old. The minister had preached a great sermon, and people were responding. Many of them were crying as they stood or knelt at the altar. I didn't understand why everyone was so emotional. My mother explained, "Everybody's either going through something, coming out of something, or getting ready for something. And they all know that the answer is Jesus." He was the answer for those who had made it through, for those going through, and for those getting ready.

When my mother said that, I knew in my heart that Jesus really had walked this earth. I knew in my heart that He was Lord and that God had raised Him from the dead. At the time I probably couldn't have articulated it quite like that, but I knew He was real, His way was the best way to live, and He was the answer to anything I encountered.

Knowing that Jesus is the answer makes you a Believer.

CHAPTER 6

Trials, Traps, and Victories

Some fell on rocky places,
where it did not have much soil.
—JESUS OF NAZARETH (MATTHEW 13:5)

Becoming a Believer doesn't exempt you from the process of growth in spiritual maturity, which necessarily involves trials, traps, and times of victory. Remember, God isn't looking for perfection; He is looking for order. He wants you to follow the order He has established. The life of a Believer includes its share of trials. Those trials are the means by which you grow as faith gets more of you and you get more of faith.

THE TRIALS OF A BELIEVER

When an Unbeliever first becomes a Believer, he doesn't know what it means to believe. He knows only *that* he believes. He knows that Jesus, who is the Lord of the universe, is also his Savior. He knows that God raised Jesus from the dead. And at the start that might be all a new Believer knows.

Every one of us learns what it means to be a Believer by living in relationship with other Believers who are more mature spiritually. They are, in order of maturity, an Example, a Teacher, and an Imparter. A Believer learns how to follow Jesus through everyday life experience, through teachable moments that God brings, through mentoring, and through prayer and Bible study. Spiritual growth comes gradually, so a new Believer needs to know it will take time to learn and to grow in faith. When a Believer has other Christians investing in her life, along with prayer and the Scriptures, the Holy Spirit is free to work. God's Spirit will open a Believer's eyes and instill in her life the qualities needed to grow into maturity in Christ.

Teachable moments serve two primary purposes. First, they teach Believers what it means to be followers of Jesus. Second, teachable moments are the means used by the Holy Spirit to help Believers confront and overcome the patterns of practice, decision, and attitude they learned when they were Unbelievers.

What it means to believe

The first of a Believer's trials are designed to teach us what it means to believe. These trials push Believers beyond their comfort zone. So if you are a new Believer and you're being challenged by God in a way that takes you to an uncomfortable place, you're right where you're supposed to be. Anyone who has grown at all in Christ has had those experiences. Some of mine came at a young age.

As I mentioned earlier, I've been playing football since I was a child. I did well as a young boy, but when I reached high school, people started noticing my performance on the field. Local sports reporters picked up on it and began following my school's games.

The week following a big victory, some of my teammates were talking about the game and the attention we were attracting from the media. My aunt Gene told me that when I talked to reporters after our next game,

I should make sure I gave God the credit and the glory for my athletic ability and the good result on the field. I knew she was right, but the thought of speaking so openly to a sportswriter about God made me uncomfortable. Still, I took Aunt Gene's words to heart. She wasn't just an aunt; she was my grandmother's sister, my great-aunt. And more than that, she was a mentor and a guide to me and almost everyone in my family. When she told me I should give God the glory for my success, I knew I had to find a way to act on her counsel.

The following Friday my team played one of our biggest rivals. I ran well as a ballcarrier and scored four touchdowns. Afterward, news reporters were waiting to interview me as I came off the field. When they asked what I thought about the game, I said in a shy voice, "I thank God for this game."

When I saw Aunt Gene later that week, she said, "Did you do it? Did you give God the glory for what happened?"

"Yes ma'am," I replied. "I did."

"Good," she said with a smile. "Do it next week and watch what happens."

The next week we played another important rival, and I scored five touchdowns. When reporters approached me after the game, I was a little bolder to speak up and give God the credit. As we left the locker room, I saw Aunt Gene standing with my mother. She asked me again, "Did you do it? Did you give God the glory?"

"Yes ma'am," I replied. "I did it."

She had a big smile on her face. "When you give God praise, He always shows up." Then she challenged me: "Shaun, do it again and watch what happens."

The next game was tough. We started slowly, and the other team, Lexington-Lafayette High School, played hard. At the end of the first quarter the score was tied 7–7. Our team had scored a touchdown, but it was one of my best friends, Brian Maney, who had crossed the goal line for us. As we moved into the second quarter, the game picked up, and Boone County High School began to roll. We went on to win by a score of 81–7. That night I scored seven touchdowns.

As my team walked off the field, a reporter approached me. This time I was ready and eager to speak up about what God had done in my life. The cameraman flipped on the light, and I screamed, "God's the Man!"

Standing there in front of sportswriters and a crowd of parents and my fellow students, I explained how my aunt had told me that speaking about God and giving Him praise, glory, and credit for your talent allows the most amazing things to happen. It makes it possible for people to hear about God who otherwise might not have a chance to hear about His power. When a Believer gives testimony to what God is doing, it makes it possible for ears to hear, minds to understand, and lives to change.

The experience of standing in front of my teammates, friends from school, parents, and the news media and talking so boldly about God stretched me into uncomfortable places. I didn't like speaking up that way and being publicly identified as a Believer. It's not that I doubted my faith. I was a Christian, and serving God was first in my heart. But when you stand up like that in public, people tend to give you a label. They start assuming things about you that are false, and they discount much of who you are before they even get to know you. I was me, and I wanted to be the *me* God had created me to be. Not the *me* someone else thought I ought to be or a person they wrongly assumed I was.

As I wrestled with that, God did not condemn me for my hesitancy. He already knew how awkward I felt. That's the reason He brought me to that experience. I don't know if the words I said to the reporters made any difference in anyone else's life, but giving God credit made a big difference in *my* life, and that was the point God wanted to lead me to.

The value of being stretched

Just like the growing pains you experience when you are young, growing as a Believer is a stretching experience. It feels awkward, and it demands you say and do things that don't come naturally. But living through those stretching experiences grows you into a deeper understanding of what it means to follow Christ. God is not trying to bust you. He's trying to teach you and show you the things of the faith you don't know about.

I heard about a guy in New York who works with drug addicts and alcoholics out of a ministry facility in a tough section of Brooklyn. Part of the work is done through a residential program. Guys come there to physically detoxify, then they live there in a discipling relationship with their counselors. As part of the program, they conduct a worship service every Sunday. The service is open to family members of the guys in the program and to people who live in the community.

One Sunday as one of the counselors was preaching and leading the worship service, he noticed a woman sitting up front. She lived in the neighborhood but never had attended their services before. As the worship service moved into preaching, he noticed she was nodding her head and agreeing with what he was saying. He warmed to his topic and grew more animated. With each phrase the woman nodded her head, and he heard her say, "(Bleep) right, Preacher. (Bleep) right." He kept preaching, and she kept agreeing. "Go ahead on, Preacher. (Bleep) right. (Bleep) right."

The preacher had never heard such language spoken so openly in a worship service. The woman was a new convert, and the other worshipers were glad to see her attend services. At first, to avoid offending her, no one talked to her about her inappropriate language. When someone did finally talk to her about it, they found out she wasn't offended at all. She had been raised around that kind of language and thought nothing of using words of that nature. She didn't know that her language was inappropriate, either in worship or in everyday conversation.

Breaking down strongholds

Trials can be the work of the Holy Spirit in tearing down the spiritual strongholds that developed around decisions and practices of people's life when they were Unbelievers. Those strongholds often involve sensual conduct they witnessed or participated in early in life. When you engage in those activities outside of God's established order, you move outside His boundaries. God designed sexual activity for marriage alone and only with your spouse. He established those limits for our protection. Enjoying sex within the context of marriage is a wonderful and beautiful thing. But having that same experience outside the context of marriage is destructive. It becomes a habit, and before you know it, the habit has formed the core of a stronghold from which Satan raids your soul and your spirit.

Allowing God to tear down such strongholds is often as simple as renouncing the underlying practice. The first miracle recorded in the gospel of Mark is Jesus' driving an evil spirit out of a person's life. To do that, He simply said, "Be quiet!" and "Come out of him!" (Mark 1:25). When faced with continual temptation to sin, you can speak to the temptation in the same way by saying, "Be quiet and go away!" Satan is an accuser, and when he confronts you, he roars like a lion. He tells you all the bad things that are going to happen in an attempt to intimidate you. In truth, he will leave you alone if you just tell him to go away (see James 4:7 and 2 Corinthians 10:4–5).

Habits and strongholds that formed early in your life, the ones with roots that run back to childhood, deform your life. They twist your personality and character. Some of the scars will remain, since all actions have consequences. But as you mature as a Believer, God takes the battered parts of your personality and character and turns them into things of beauty. In a way only possible through the Holy Spirit, He takes your sin-scarred personality and transforms it according to His will. He makes you the person He created you to be, regardless of what you did in your previous life as an Unbeliever.

"The stone the builders rejected has become the capstone" (Matthew 21:42, quoting Psalm 118:22) isn't only a proclamation about Jesus; it's a statement about how God works in our lives. When we yield ourselves to Him and to the working of His Spirit, He takes the things we despise most about ourselves and turns them into the most attractive parts of who we are.

THE TRAPS OF A BELIEVER

Believers often commit their lives to Christ thinking that everything is complete, that by becoming a Believer, they have become all that they need to be. Meanwhile, they continue living in sin and don't know it. Then, when they discover the sin in their lives, Satan lies to them in an attempt to defeat them. He tells them they're stuck and they can't escape the sin.

"Aha! You shouldn't have done that," he says. "You are the lowest of sinners. No one else thinks those shameful things or does things like that, and you sure can't tell anyone." Those are lies from the pit of hell, and as a Believer, you have to reject them. Believers live by God's truth and resist the lies of Satan.

Satan tailors the lies he tells you, based on the things you struggled with as an Unbeliever. He traps young Believers by using the things that snagged them in their past life. If you used to struggle with drugs, alcohol, sexual immorality, lust, or greed, Satan will make those same things look attractive to you now. He will use your weakness to lure you, but when you actually taste those things again, you find they are bitter and ugly. Still, they can gain a foothold in your life at a deeper level than you realize. Left unattended, they warp your personality and become habits that control you.

For several years I have mentored groups of young men across the country, showing them what it means to be a Believer. I have a unique relationship with each of these groups. Some of them meet almost exclusively for Bible study. Others just hang out, talking and spending time together. It depends largely on their personality types and where the men are with the Lord. We attend football or basketball games and other events together, or I have them over to my house. I take some of them with me to my speaking engagements and let them dive right in with ministry.

Discipling people isn't just about giving out information. It's about giving them an *experience* along with the information. You can't merely talk to a disciple; you have to invest your life in a disciple's life. To do that, you have to be willing to listen without judging. Doing that will let you get close enough to a person so you can effect changes in his or her life. Investing your life in a young Believer will stretch your faith and bring you into some interesting situations.

I mentored a young man named Lucas. When I first met him, he was a young Believer. After a while he started hanging out with other men who said they were Believers too. This group got together one Friday night to play cards, and as they were playing, they began drinking. Sometime that evening Lucas raised the question, "Is this right? Should we be drinking?"

Everyone at the table responded with a hearty, "Yeah. Sure. It's okay. We're Christians. We aren't causing anyone to stumble."

I know you've heard those same comments. Perhaps you've even said these things about drinking or some other behavior. As you might expect, before the card game ended, they had all gotten drunk. They knew enough not to drive home while intoxicated, and besides, they didn't want anyone to know they'd been drinking. So they slept over at the house where they'd been playing cards.

The next Friday they met again to play cards. Once again they started drinking. As before, they all got drunk and slept over at the house rather than go home intoxicated. Soon the card game and excessive drinking became a ritual. This went on for a while.

One day Lucas and I had a heart-to-heart session. I do this periodically with the guys I disciple. We meet one-on-one so I can catch up with them and see how they're doing. Everyone needs accountability, and new Believers need a lot of it. I try to give them more than enough.

While Lucas and I were talking, he asked, "Is drunkenness different in God's eyes when you're only drunk around other Believers?"

I said, "What do you mean?"

He told me what had been happening. Then he asked again, "Is it different in God's eyes if you're doing it around other Believers? Not any Unbelievers there, just Believers."

I gave him a wry smile. "What do you think?"

"I don't know." He shrugged. "I guess when you're drunk, you're drunk."

We turned to Scripture, and I walked him through some passages that show that God has given us clear commands regarding the consumption of alcohol. The point in telling this story is not to tell you not to drink. The important thing is to study what God requires of us, then to live accordingly. Lucas and I looked at Proverbs 23:29–35; 31:4–7; Isaiah 5:11–16; and Ephesians 5:18.

I told him, "At the end of the day, we know that being drunk is a sin. We also know that to deliberately sin is to reject God and the sacrifice that Jesus made. You have to choose what you'll do when you're with friends who play cards and drink. But if you stop drinking with them, two things will happen. One, you will honor God by your decision. And two, you will affect the life of at least one other person who is in that card game, because I know he is thinking about it too."

Lucas saw my point, but he pressed me on the question of drinking. "Do you think it's wrong to even drink?"

"Lucas, you have to go with the convictions in your heart," I told him. "We can discuss theology and laws all week. But each of us has to hear God and then obey. The calling on my life is bigger than a law. I don't think it's right for anyone to drink if they are going to represent Christ. Not because one drink might get them drunk, but because that one drink might cause someone else to drink. And I don't want to be the one who opens up that door for them."

In some churches, people would look at Lucas and suggest he never was a Believer in the first place. They assume that a true Believer doesn't ever drink alcohol. Other Christians would classify him as a backslider. Some would say he had fallen from grace, the evidence being that he went along with the drinking. But nothing could be further from the truth.

Lucas is a Believer. He knows that Jesus is Lord, and at the time we were discussing his questions, he knew that God had raised Jesus from the dead. He just didn't always know what that meant in terms of everyday life and the choices he needed to make. That he fell victim to the error of others who claimed to be Believers is somewhat understandable, but it's important to see the danger in that. That error opened him to yet another trap: the trap of becoming *lukewarm.*

If Satan can't get a young Believer to reject Christ and the gospel, he will use a different approach. Satan will entice a young Believer to water down his or her beliefs. Not being as bad as someone else isn't the same as living in obedience to God. As Satan works to dilute the power and effectiveness of God's Word in a Believer's life, often he will do what he did to Lucas. He brings a Believer into relationships with people who tear down rather than build up. This is what the men in the card game were doing. There are people who want to live as close to the line of sin as possible while still justifying what they're doing. And when you do that, you leave yourself wide open to a trap.

THE VICTORIES OF A BELIEVER

The victory for Believers comes when their lifestyle, character, and personality start to reflect more of Christ and less of themselves. I'm not talking about attaining perfection but rather grasping for more of Christ.

Many of the things new Believers encounter in Christian circles revolve around avoiding certain behaviors. Don't look at pornography, don't get drunk, don't smoke, don't cuss, and don't be sexually immoral. It's necessary to break certain behavior patterns from the past, but as you mature in Christ, you start to shift your focus from "don't" to "do." Love God. Serve Him with all your heart. Love your neighbor. Care for the poor. Forgive those who hurt you, and do it without being asked. Forgive in advance those who you know are going to hurt you. Let go of the rights you've clung to all your life—the right to be treated well, the right to have your own way, and the right to get mad when things don't go your way. Get rid of the right to be materialistic and only think about yourself and the right to put yourself first and take care of your own concerns before you help others. Make the shift in perspective, from avoiding the "don't" to doing the "do." That is the victory of the Believer.

Rules have their place as a starting point, but they become less important as you mature spiritually. Rules provide the minimum requirements. They tell you the least you can do and still qualify. Building codes, electrical codes, safety codes, theological codes—they all do the same thing. They tell you where the line is and how far you can go before you cross it. That's what happens when you focus on the "don'ts" of loving God. It locks your focus on the minimum requirements. All you're thinking about is the least you can do to still behave like one of God's children.

Changing your perspective from the "don'ts" to the "dos" moves your attention from the minimum requirements to the maximum potential. The God of all creation wants to know you. That relationship has infinite potential. Reaching the depths of it is a wonderful journey in which He becomes real to you every moment of every day.

Victory for Believers comes as we understand that being a Christian shows in the way we live and think and in the kinds of decisions we make. With that victory, Jesus is not merely the hope of the ages but the Believer's own personal hope and the Person around whom we orient our entire life. At that point, when Believers choose not to do something, it's not motivated by a desire to obey a rule. They choose against doing something because they love Jesus.

I remember my mother's sitting my older brother Durran and me down one day for a family talk. She said, "Boys, you're getting to the age where I can't scare you into doing the right things with discipline and punishment. So from now on I'm going to ask you to do things right simply because you love me and I said so." We were shocked, but we understood. Then she said, "I'd much rather you do things right because you love me."

That's how Jesus feels about our actions. He gets the greatest pleasure when our conduct is motivated by our love for Him. When Believers reach that point, they become Examples. (We will take a closer look at the life of an Example in chapter 8.)

CHAPTER 7

Peter as a Believer

Tell me to come to you on the water.
—SIMON PETER (MATTHEW 14:28)

While working on this book, I was looking in a thesaurus for synonyms of the word *believer.* Four words jumped off the page: convert, disciple, supporter, and follower. The convert is one who goes through life thinking one way and then finds a brand-new way of thinking. Peter, one of the twelve apostles, had a brother named Andrew. Andrew had been listening to the preaching of John the Baptist, who directed him to Jesus. Andrew then brought his brother, Peter, to meet Jesus—and nothing was the same after that. When Peter put down his fishing nets and followed Jesus, he became a convert (see John 1:35–42).

A Believer is converted from a past way of life into a completely new way of living. A disciple is a Believer who goes through strict training under the guidance of a Teacher for the purpose of learning the skills of the Teacher. That process of learning is also a process of change, as the disciple is transformed. Jesus trained His disciples by demonstrating before them the things of God. They saw the life He lived and experienced the miracles He performed. Under Jesus' watchful eye, they grew and matured in their understanding and slowly came to be like Him. Thus, the disciples become like their Teacher.

Then one day Jesus sent the disciples out in groups of two with a charge to do themselves what He had been doing. Only this time He didn't go with them. He sent them out on their own.

> Take nothing for the journey except a staff—no bread, no bag, no money in your belts. Wear sandals but not an extra tunic. Whenever you enter a house, stay there until you leave that town. And if any place will not welcome you or listen to you, shake the dust off your feet when you leave, as a testimony against them. (Mark 6:8–11)

When you think about what the disciples did, it really seems incredible. They went into the countryside of Israel, among their fellow Jews, and preached that the Messiah had come. They didn't go into the Bible Belt and invite friendly listeners to attend a Bible study. The people they spoke to had not already decided that Jesus of Nazareth was the Messiah. And being monotheistic, they certainly didn't buy the idea that Jesus, a man, was God in human flesh. Instead, many of them thought Jesus was a heretic. So the disciples, preaching the gospel message, had been given a tough assignment.

And what happened? Scripture says, "They went out and preached that people should repent. They drove out many demons and anointed many sick people with oil and healed them" (Mark 6:12–13).

A time will come when you will face a similar circumstance. You will receive a leading from the Holy Spirit to go to a particular place and begin a particular work for God. And you will go with no guarantee that anything you do will meet with success. You will experience doubts, and fear will crouch around every corner. Even some of the people who know you well will suggest that you should wait for a more opportune time, wait until there's enough money to cover the budget, wait until you can find a more responsive audience. But if you are a disciple of Jesus, you know that your life is committed to obeying the Master, Jesus. So you step out in faith, knowing that He will make a way where there is no way.

A supporter (another meaning of *believer*) is one who helps another's cause. Supporters are similar to Peter when he helped Jesus feed the five thousand. Peter gathered the loaves and fishes and organized the crowd into groups. I'm sure he wondered how Jesus would feed so many people, and he perhaps questioned why Jesus would even try. Still, Peter did as he was told. Imagine how he felt as he collected the leftovers after the meal (see Mark 6:30–44). Peter supported the work of his Master and was blessed by the miracle that Jesus performed.

A follower trails behind another; he copies another. A follower watches what the master is doing, and then he or she does the same thing. Jesus wanted His disciples to do more than merely copy what He did, but as you look through the New Testament, you'll see there is a great deal of similarity between what Jesus did and what His disciples did after the resurrection. Notice the similarity between what Jesus did in healing Jairus's daughter (see Mark 5:35–43) and what Peter did in healing a woman named Dorcas who lived in Joppa (see Acts 9:36–43).

The Healing of Jairus's Daughter (Mark 5:35–43)

While Jesus was still speaking, some men came from the house of Jairus, the synagogue ruler. "Your daughter is dead," they said. "Why bother the teacher any more?"

Ignoring what they said, Jesus told the synagogue ruler, "Don't be afraid; just believe."

He did not let anyone follow him except Peter, James and John the brother of James. When they came to the home of the synagogue ruler, Jesus saw a commotion, with people crying and

wailing loudly. He went in and said to them, "Why all this commotion and wailing? The child is not dead but asleep." But they
laughed at him.

After he put them all out, he took the child's father and
mother and the disciples who were with him, and went in where
the child was. He took her by the hand and said to her, *"Talitha
koum!"* (which means, "Little girl, I say to you, get up!"). Immediately the girl stood up and walked around (she was twelve years
old). At this they were completely astonished. He gave strict orders not to let anyone know about this, and told them to give her
something to eat.

The Healing of Dorcas (Acts 9:36–43)

In Joppa there was a disciple named Tabitha (which, when translated, is Dorcas), who was always doing good and helping the
poor. About that time she became sick and died, and her body
was washed and placed in an upstairs room. Lydda was near
Joppa; so when the disciples heard that Peter was in Lydda, they
sent two men to him and urged him, "Please come at once!"

Peter went with them, and when he arrived he was taken upstairs to the room. All the widows stood around him, crying and
showing him the robes and other clothing that Dorcas had made
while she was still with them.

Peter sent them all out of the room; then he got down on his
knees and prayed. Turning toward the dead woman, he said,
"Tabitha, get up." She opened her eyes, and seeing Peter she sat
up. He took her by the hand and helped her to her feet. Then he
called the believers and the widows and presented her to them

alive. This became known all over Joppa, and many people believed in the Lord. Peter stayed in Joppa for some time with a tanner named Simon.

In both instances the person who needed ministry was already dead! When Jesus arrived at Jairus's house, He made everyone leave the room except for Peter, James, and John. In Joppa, Peter did the same by sending everyone from the room. Jesus knelt and prayed. Peter did too. And when Jesus finished praying, He said to Jairus's daughter, "Little girl, I say to you, get up" (Mark 5:41). Likewise, Peter said to Dorcas, "Tabitha, get up" (Acts 9:40).

Peter experienced many dramatic moments with Jesus, moments when he learned to emulate his Master. One of those moments came late one night on the Sea of Galilee after the feeding of the five thousand. Jesus had preached all day and then fed the huge crowd. Late that afternoon He sent the disciples ahead by boat to the opposite side. In the middle of the night, Jesus came to them, walking on the water. The disciples saw Him coming and were afraid. To relieve their fear, Jesus called out to them.

"Take courage. It is I. Don't be afraid."

"Lord, if it is you," Peter replied, "tell me to come to you on the water." (Matthew 14:27–28)

Jesus was pleased by Peter's response. One of His star pupils wanted to get out of the boat and defy the laws of physics. Peter was saying, by asking to come to Jesus, that he believed Jesus had the power to overcome all that was known about the universe. In spite of all the evidence and a lifetime's worth of experience, Peter wanted to join Jesus in a stroll across the water. At last one of the Twelve was catching on to what Jesus meant, that they *could* do what He was doing, that they *would* do what He was doing, that they *should* do what He was doing.

Believers experience victory when they finally realize, at a level far deeper than mere faith, that Jesus is the hope of the world and also the hope of every Believer. Believers experience victory when they know without a doubt that every word that came from Jesus was true, and is true, and will come to pass both in history and in the Believer's personal life.

When you achieve that victory, like Peter, you will move to the next stage. You will become an Example.

PART 3

The Example

I bless you because you have considered
me worthy of this day and hour, that I might
receive a place among the number of the
martyrs in the cup of your Christ, to the
resurrection to eternal life, both of soul
and of body, in the incorruptibility of the
Holy Spirit.

—*THE MARTYRDOM OF POLYCARP*

Let's go for it. Let's go to the point of no
return…. When you cross the line you
become a dangerous person.

—BANNING LIEBSCHER, JESUS CULTURE,
REDDING, CALIFORNIA

CHAPTER 8

Becoming an Example

To do like Jesus and turn the tables
To give it all to get nothing back.
—JASON UPTON, "IT AIN'T EASY"

xamples are Believers who have matured spiritually. They have learned from Christ and followed Him, and now they are at the place where their life reflects more of Christ and less of themselves. They started out as Wanderers, then began asking the questions of the Wonderer, and then were converted to Christ. Their way of thinking and living changed when they became Believers.

As Believers learn from Jesus, much more changes than just what they believe. Their approach to the world changes, their minds are changed, and the way they live changes. They submit their will to the Lord's will, and their lifestyle shows more of the character of Christ. The Believers' life exhibits love, joy, peace, patience, kindness, goodness, gentleness, faithfulness, and self-control—the fruit of the Spirit. Their life reflects the ways of the Holy Spirit and less of what Paul called the "flesh"—greed, selfishness, envy, and the like. They no longer live at the line of mediocrity, doing only the minimum and living as close to sin as possible. Instead, they live continually in the presence of God.

That is a brief description of the Example, a person who has allowed the Holy Spirit to gain control over his or her thoughts and actions. As you walk with the Holy Spirit from the Believer stage into the Example stage, the process follows a progression outlined in 2 Peter.

> For this very reason, make every effort to add to your faith good-ness; and to goodness, knowledge; and to knowledge, self-control; and to self-control, perseverance; and to perseverance, godliness; and to godliness, brotherly kindness; and to brotherly kindness, love. (1:5–7)

ADD TO YOUR FAITH...GOODNESS

Much of what our society defines as good or bad has nothing to do with moral absolutes. Things that were prohibited on television in the 1950s are now commonplace. Divorce was once taboo, but now it is tolerated and widely accepted, even in the most conservative churches.

The ability to differentiate between right and wrong, good and bad, lies at the core of the human conscience. It is the basis upon which we begin to grow as Christians, but it is only the beginning. When a person is converted from Wonderer to Believer, he or she is acting on faith. The Holy Spirit continues to work in the new Believer's life, showing him or her what is of God and what isn't. Knowing right from wrong is the point from which a Believer commences the journey. And as a Believer grows into an Example, it is necessary to add to one's faith.

When Scripture speaks of adding "to your faith goodness," it isn't talking about goodness as defined by popular culture. It is talking about goodness as defined by God—a concept He introduced from the be-ginning when He looked at creation and said, "It is good."[1] Good is a reflection of God's character and nature. Anything that does not con-form to His character is bad. God is good, and His goodness is available to us.

Taste and see that the LORD is good;
>   blessed is the man who takes refuge in
>   him. (Psalm 34:8)

The goodness of God is foundational to all other teaching. Understanding that concept, believing it, and having it ingrained deep in your mind, heart, soul, and spirit are essential for the walk of faith. Doubting God's goodness not only opens you to attack from the enemy; it clouds your thoughts and makes you susceptible to deception. In the creation story, Adam and Eve were susceptible to the serpent's lies because they doubted that God really meant good toward them. They harbored a suspicion that He was depriving them of something wonderful. In truth, God had restricted them in only one way: to not eat from the Tree of the Knowledge of Good and Evil. In all other ways, they were free to live as they wanted. And His one restriction on their lives was given for their protection. Had they trusted in God's goodness, they might never have fallen from grace and been banished from the garden.

It's understandable that many people would be confused by words such as *good* and *bad* since our culture does not support biblical morality. But God does not expect you to simply accept the notion of His goodness; He invites you to *experience* that goodness. Those experiences come through the circumstances of life. They may seem scary at times, but they are designed by God to instill in you absolute faith in His goodness.

I remember my good friend Judah Smith telling about visiting a cheese factory on a church youth-group trip when he was twelve years old. He thought touring a factory was horrible. There were twenty-five kids walking through a cheese factory for *hours*. He winced at the memory as he told me about the people who worked there explaining all the varieties of cheese and the way they were made. The workers were excited to describe all the varieties and went on at length about cheddar,

American, and provolone. "It got so bad," Judah said, "that I became a pouting kid."

At the end of the tour, the workers brought all the boys some fresh cheese to taste. Judah was still sulking and refused to eat. But as he watched his friends enjoying the cheese, he began to wonder if he should try it. So he did. As the cheese touched his tongue, his taste buds exploded. He ate so much that he began to negotiate for a summer job at the factory.

Many people look at God and the things of God as they would an unwanted tour of a cheese factory. They look around at churches or at other Christians and think *boring*. Some actually get close enough to smell the goodness of God, but as the wind shifts, the scent blows in another direction. Then they forget about God and what He offers them, while others actually taste the goodness of God, and they are never the same again (see Psalm 34:8).

ADD TO GOODNESS...KNOWLEDGE

The next step in the process is to add knowledge to goodness. God wants to instill in you the character qualities described in the fruit of the Spirit. And for that to happen, you need knowledge—knowledge of Scripture, knowledge about the Holy Spirit, and knowledge of yourself.

Scripture is the record of God's revelation to men and women in the past, and it is His way of speaking to us today. There are a number of ways to read it. I'll share a few of the ways I approach Scripture, all of which can help you gain knowledge of God's Word.

Sometimes a particular story pops into my mind, and I read through that for a while. Focusing on a particular incident in Scripture often leads to intense study of a specific time in the history of God's people. Many of the events in the Bible occurred over a period of only a few days. Studying those stories and the events surrounding them allows you to put them in a broader context.

At other times I read an entire book of the Bible, chapter by chapter, underlining anything that stands out to me. Reading a book from beginning to end allows you to recognize broader themes of how God worked in the past across different generations of His followers.

The third way I approach Scripture is by studying a particular person. I track his or her life, looking for hidden lessons, examples, and experiences that will help me grow. The Bible also has interesting ideas buried in unusual places, particularly in the genealogical sections that we tend to skip over.

A fourth way to read the Bible is to study a specific word or topic. I like to take a keyword and check every place in Scripture where that word occurs. Meanings of words sometimes change over time, so comparing the use of a word in one context with its use in another can be confusing. But it also can be enlightening. The God who spoke to the men and women of old is the same God who came to us in Jesus. Studying words across the full range of biblical revelation can give us a glimpse of how God acts to bring about His will on earth.

The fifth way I approach Scripture is by studying notes from a sermon I heard or a Bible study I attended. Or sometimes it's a verse someone else discussed that intrigued me. Using their ideas often opens up new ways of seeing familiar scriptures.

Regardless of how you approach it, gaining knowledge of the Scriptures will transform your life. It's like washing the dirt from your spirit and mind. It should be done daily.

Add knowledge...of the Holy Spirit

While the Holy Spirit reveals things about people and events recorded in Scripture, He also reveals things about Himself. He isn't standing over you with a hammer, waiting to crack you on the head when you make a mistake. In fact, He isn't all that concerned about your mistakes. He's concerned about the lesson He is presenting to you at that particular moment.

Earlier I told you about how my aunt challenged me to acknowledge God in my postgame interviews when I was in high school. She encouraged me to give God the praise and glory for my success on the field. At that time a thousand other things were going on in my life, some of them not all that great, certainly not for one who claimed to be following Christ. I realize now that God wasn't too concerned about the other things I was involved in. If He *had* been, He would have started working on those issues in my life. But instead, He turned me toward publicly acknowledging Him. Doing that not only brought the reward of obedience, which was made obvious on the playing field, but it also turned me toward God in a new and exciting way. By my response of obedience, God not only was able to stretch my understanding of Him, but He also was able to gently turn me away from many of the things that were tugging me in the opposite direction. He was more interested in doing that than in receiving my pitiful praise. Praising Him and acknowledging Him publicly were the means by which He guided me in His direction. He wanted me—my entire life and my full commitment—not my legalistic obedience to a list of rules.

Listening for the still, small voice of God as opposed to following a written plan or program is not always comfortable, and sometimes it's a little scary. But God still speaks to us, and we can hear Him. (The Holy Spirit speaks to you with a voice that sounds like your voice, but the problem is, so does your flesh. Sorting that out requires an unvarying standard, and Scripture provides that standard. If you think you've heard God, but you test the message against the fruit of the Spirit, and it doesn't match, then you didn't hear God.)

Several times already I've mentioned the fruit of the Holy Spirit. The

list Paul provides in Galatians 5:22–23 is a list of God's character qualities. When you hear a voice that you think belongs to God, or you receive
direction you think is from God, compare what you hear to those character traits. God's leading for you will *always* align with those qualities.

The second way you can distinguish God's voice from your own
thoughts is through comparing what you hear to the places in Scripture
where God has spoken on that same topic. Earlier I told you about Lucas,
the young Believer who attended a Friday-night card game with other "Believers" and began drinking with them. He sensed that what they were
doing was wrong. That inner sense was the Holy Spirit trying to guide
him away from alcohol and away from those who would lead him down
that path. When Lucas and I discussed the matter, we compared what his
friends were doing with what Scripture says on the subject. The Bible is
clear that drinking to excess and drunkenness are sin (see Proverbs 23:29–
35; 31:4–7; Isaiah 5:11–16; Ephesians 5:18). Lucas had been hearing the
Holy Spirit's voice; he just wasn't too comfortable with what he heard.

Add knowledge...of yourself

As the Holy Spirit reveals more about Scripture and about Himself, He
also reveals more about you. This kind of growth can be uncomfortable
and sometimes even painful, but it is essential if you want to continue
growing in spiritual maturity. Gaining knowledge about yourself is like
peeling an onion—no single layer goes all the way to the core. Yet slowly,
methodically, God finds a beginning point and peels away layers, forcing
you to face more and more of yourself, working toward the core of your
personality and character. At the core lie strongholds that Satan established around the traps you fell into as an Unbeliever. They are the root
of the recurring sin in your life, the areas where sin has become a habit.
God has to get to those strongholds and tear them down in order to set
you free.

When the peeling process reaches the core of who you are, it can bring you to tears. When God shows you who you really are, the knowledge pushes you to a new level of understanding, taking you deeper and deeper into God and deeper into yourself. The journey goes in both directions at the same time. God reveals Himself to you, and He reveals you to yourself.

God commonly uses memories to reveal things about yourself. The Holy Spirit knows exactly what happened to you in the past—the places you went, whom you were with, what you did and said, and the things that happened to you. Often He brings to mind some of your long-forgotten memories and uses them to show you important things about yourself. As He does this, He shows you the beginning points of the troubles you face now.

When you were a Wanderer or a Wonderer, Satan influenced you with lies. He lied about who you are and who God is, and he lied about the things that would bring you fun, pleasure, and fulfillment. You believed some of the lies, and you lived your life as if the lies were true. No devils dressed in red appeared at your side and shoved a contract in front of you. Nor did they offer you riches in exchange for your soul. In real life Satan's work is much more subtle and harder to identify.

If you're a male, think back to when you were a young boy. An older kid down the street tells you what he and his friend did to a girl living in an apartment in the neighborhood. He tells the story in such a way that you feel this is what a man does, that it's the way it's supposed to be when a boy grows older. You believe that once you reach a certain age, you and your friends had better have a sex story to tell, or other guys will think something is wrong. When you decide this is the path you will take, you are allowing a lie to guide your life.

It builds from there. The older boy's stories fuel your imagination. From there, your curiosity leads you to explore pornographic magazines or Web sites. The images you see and the words you read tell you more lies. They say, "This is exciting, and it's exactly how it's supposed to be." When you agree with that lie, the lie becomes a part of you. You are involving your heart in an agreement with Satan.

Or let's say you're a woman or teenage girl. You have read romance novels and teen magazines and watched movies and television shows. You've seen how other women use their looks and their bodies to attract attention. And you have come to believe that flirting, dressing in revealing clothing, and making it known that you are available is the way to get the attention you crave. You accepted the lie that says the most desirable men won't pay attention to you if you dress modestly and have integrity with your words and actions. You compromised your standards and started dressing and acting provocatively. Satan told you that you'd be happy with the attention. But sadly, that lie of Satan helps form your character and personality, and eventually it will become your new identity. It can turn you into a woman who announces that she's okay with being treated like an object. Many girls and women have given away everything they truly want as women because their hearts agreed to this lie.

Identifying Satan's lies

Satan is smooth. If he showed up looking like a demon out of a horror movie, you'd run the other way. So, instead, he comes in the form of lust-inducing images on a Web site or a fantasy story in a book. Before long, the messages of the fantasy images and the fantasy stories have entered your mind. You start thinking that sex outside marriage is acceptable. The urge is undeniable, and you rationalize that it can't be resisted. You start to think you *deserve* the pleasure and excitement.

Friends might try to steer you back toward God and sexual morality, but you believe they only want to rob you of the fulfillment you seek.

You decide they have no right to judge you, so you reject their help. You ignore their counsel that the path of worldly pleasure will only make you desire more pleasure. When you accept the lies of Satan, that traps your mind and changes your life.

There are other lies that shape you, and they are lies you never chose to accept. When you were growing up, people close to you conveyed messages about the world and your place in it, as well as messages about who you are. The weight of those lies stayed with you into adulthood. When you were a kid, you made honest mistakes. Let's say you accidentally kicked over a can of paint, and it spilled on a new hardwood floor. Someone you trusted—a parent or other relative—shouted at you, "How stupid can you be? Didn't you see that can sitting right there in front of you? Look what you did to my beautiful floor!"

As you grew up and made other innocent mistakes, you heard the same message: "You're clumsy and thoughtless. How can you still be so stupid?" Before long, you started to agree with the lie. *I really am stupid. I'm worthless. I can't do anything right.* You signed Satan's contract.

Here's a lie that hits close to home for anyone trying to support a family. It's a week before payday, and you have five dollars left from your last paycheck. You have four kids to feed, and you're worried about how you'll make it. Before long, thoughts crowd your mind. *We're going to run out of groceries. God doesn't care what happens to us. He must be mad at me. He probably won't even listen to me anymore.* Those statements are lies.

When you give in to lies, you're opening yourself to worry and fear. Before long, you aren't thinking about God's goodness or His promises to you. All you can think about is how alone you are and how terrible your circumstances are. Fear strangles everything that faith has given you. When you agree with the lie of fear, you're asking Satan to take charge.

You never did sign anything in blood, but you signed a contract with

Satan every time you accepted one of his lies about you or about God. He takes the agreements you made with him and builds a stronghold, getting a grip on some aspect of your life. He only takes a small part at first, but he gets a firm grip on it. Then, working out from one stronghold, he attempts to invade other areas of your life.

Rejecting Satan's lies

You've heard stories about a young woman who grew up with strict moral standards and maintained strong convictions regarding sexual purity. She was a girl who knew who she was and what she wanted out of life. She was committed to God's best and never apologized for refusing to go along with the crowd.

But then it happened. She took her eyes off Christ and looked around at what else was being offered. She believed a lie of Satan. She listened to him saying, "You know you're curious." And she kept listening.

"You know you wonder what it's like to really cut loose."

"You know it's easy for you to attract attention."

"You know you like him—and you've been wanting to, anyway."

So she gave in. She did it. And nobody on campus or at the office could believe it happened. As a matter of fact, she had trouble believing it herself.

Sin is sin. We all fall in it daily. Each of us is vulnerable, and we're vulnerable to different temptations. Jesus' love, grace, and mercy are available to us when we confess and repent. But when a girl or young woman gives in and "does it," she is attacked with more lies. Satan doesn't stop after he causes a Believer or an Example to trip and fall. He keeps at it, telling more lies.

"You are the one who decided to do it," he whispers. "This is who you really are, a woman who can't stop giving herself away. You liked it, didn't you? Can't you see now that it wasn't that bad?"

The young woman who lost sight of her commitments and followed a lie will most likely buy into a new set of lies. The trap is set, and if she keeps buying the lies, she will be buying a new, false identity. Satan will do all he can to convince her it's too late, that she has gone too far and can never go back to a life of sexual purity.

Listen to me. That is a lie straight from the chief liar, Satan! Jesus will always take care of His children. He will always accept you right where you are, if you will only ask Him (see Luke 15:20–24). Your sin or struggle has no effect on God's love and desire for you.

Jesus loves you, and Satan lies to you, so follow what Jesus says. "The thief comes only to steal and kill and destroy; I have come that they may have life, and have it to the full" (John 10:10). The Holy Spirit knows the agreements you have made with the enemy, the times when Satan spoke a lie and you accepted it. He knows about each incident, both the conscious moments and the unconscious. You know them too; you just don't want to confront them.

This is where the Holy Spirit can work to reveal who you are at your core. The work of the Holy Spirit is often the task of bringing memories to your conscious mind and walking you back through them in a process of revelation, repentance, and renunciation. As you renounce the agreements you made with Satan, the Spirit is able to bring healing to your spirit and your soul and to set you free from the guilt and shame associated with habitual sin. Much of what He reveals to you is right there before you, often obvious to others but unseen by you.

Learning about your true self

One day my bride, Valerie, and I were watching a DVD of a sermon by Ron Carpenter Jr. He was saying that the times when you are facing an enemy are often the times your strengths and weaknesses are made apparent. He admitted that often his greatest strength was also his greatest weakness. Ron is a focused person, but his ability to focus exclusively on one thing can sometimes cause him to miss obvious things that are right under his nose.

Valerie and I, while watching Ron's sermon video, started talking about blind spots, the things we do that are obvious to others but not to ourselves.

Valerie looked at me and said, "You only reach twenty-five percent of the people you're supposed to reach."

"What?" I was so astounded I stopped the DVD. "What are you talking about?"

"I can't fully explain it, but there are people out there you purposely don't even try to connect with. You miss seventy-five percent of the people you could otherwise reach."

I asked her why she thought that, and we discussed it. After a while the conversation lagged, and we went back to the DVD. But while I watched it, I was thinking about what she had said.

Then, out of the blue, Valerie shouted, "*Rejection!* That's what it is. You have a fear of rejection!"

All at once I saw myself standing in front of an audience made up of one hundred people I know. Some were friends or associates, some were family, and some were people I had met at different functions where we crossed paths or had a conversation just one time. I noticed the crowd was divided into two groups. The fifty people on the left were not agreeing with what I was saying, while the fifty on the right were agreeing with me. Then I looked closer and noticed that the audience was divided even more. There were four groups of twenty-five, and it was clear what each group represented.

The first group, still off to the left, was the group that didn't agree with what I was saying—and I knew it. The second group of twenty-five also disagreed with me, but I did not know it.

I noticed in my heart that in the big picture, my attitude toward both groups was similar. I would shut down and disengage, but in different ways.

Moments later I saw myself flying an aircraft. I was approaching an airport with a dark storm ahead. I didn't want to go through the turbulence, so I pulled back on the steering wheel, increased the engines' power, and flew over the storm. Then the Holy Spirit spoke to me: "Shaun, this is what you do in response to the first group of twenty-five on the left. When you know someone is going to reject you, you pull back and fly right over them." I knew He was right. Whenever I met a person and knew that he or she was going to reject me, I would keep the conversation short and get out of there.

Then I saw myself driving a Jeep. The odd thing was that I kept my foot over the brake and my hand touching the emergency brake. I could tell I was looking for a reason to stop the Jeep. This is what I was doing with the second group of twenty-five once I felt their rejection after learning they did not agree with me. I would just jam on the brakes and say, "Hey, hope it works out. Got to run." Then I would be gone.

With both of the groups that didn't agree with me, I would feel the rejection and react. If I knew in advance they were going to reject me, I would fly right over them. And if I didn't know up front that they would disagree with me, I would relate to them until I sensed their rejection. Then I'd stop relating to them and shut the conversation down. Because of my attitude, I was missing the opportunity to have an impact on half the people on that side of the audience. I was limiting God's ability to minister fully through me, and I was sad to learn that about myself.

Then I looked at the fifty people in the audience to the right. The first twenty-five were some of the people whom I mentored or who mentored me. They were people who sat on the same boards and worked with some of the same organizations I worked with. I could tell they agreed with every word that came out of my mouth. I was like a pilot flying on a great, sunny day. It was smooth flying.

As I looked to the second group of twenty-five on the right, I was surprised by who was back there. I knew all one hundred people in the audience, but these twenty-five made me shake my head with amazement. I had no idea this group was listening or even paying attention, much less agreeing with me.

I was more confident with the first group of twenty-five. I knew they already agreed with me, and I was more willing to be bold and speak with passion and to invest myself in them. However, with the second group of twenty-five—the ones I didn't realize were following me—I spoke and acted passively, even about things I was passionate about. I saw myself driving the Jeep to my house, but I was driving super slow. It was like I wasn't sure how to get to my own home. I was being cautious with that group rather than bold or up-front.

God showed me that I was creating confusion for the second group. The result was that I missed out on teaching them the fullness of things that they were ready to learn. How wrong I was with them. I missed the impact I was supposed to have.

The fear of rejection is a heart issue. It is Satan's best way to prevent me from having the impact I'm supposed to have. Rejection can get into the core of who you are and affect every decision you make. My actions and attitude were the direct result of how I responded to rejection. My wrong reactions caused me to mishandle the way I connected with people, whether they were rejecting me or following me. Because of this core heart issue, I related incorrectly to seventy-five percent of the people I encountered. Valerie was right: I was reaching only twenty-five percent of the people I was supposed to reach.

But that wasn't the end of it. The Holy Spirit continued to speak to me. "What if I called you to fly *through* the storm? I never called you to avoid certain people. I never called you to shift your speech based on how people respond to what you are saying. I didn't tell you to change your attitude depending on whether you know if people are in agreement with you. And I never called you to go out and convince people to like you.

"The work I've called you to isn't about making sure that people like Shaun Alexander. It's about introducing them to Me. It's about engaging the people I bring across your path and showing them more of Me."

I knew the Holy Spirit was referring to the people I suspected were against me. I had been allowing God to use me only according to my own rules. I was controlling the flight, and if I didn't sense that people were accepting me and my message, I would go around or over them. But why did I have to know what people were thinking about me and my message? What is this avoidance of rejection all about, and where did it come from?

The more I thought about it, the more I realized that I'm not called to get the world saved. I am called to be obedient to God and to plant a seed in every life I contact. Fear of rejection was keeping me from doing that to the fullest extent possible.

Rejecting the lie of fear

It's important to get to the root of your fear, to explore the origins of your fear, so you can allow the Holy Spirit to set you free. As I mentioned earlier, memories help you on that journey. The Holy Spirit uses them to remind you of incidents in your life that you've forgotten. As I wrestled with the fear of rejection, I remembered an incident that happened when I was in fifth grade.

One of my closest friends was a boy named Jay. He and I were good athletes, and we had a lot of swagger. Our school was integrated, but most of the students were white, including Jay. One day he and I were walking down the hall, and for no apparent reason, he said, "Everybody's racist."

I laughed and said, "Everybody's not a racist."

"Yes they are," he argued, "and I hate it." To make his point, he said, "I pick on people all the time, and you are friendly to everyone. But if you asked most of them who they would rather be friends with, they'd say me because I'm white and you're black."

"That's not true," I replied.

"Yes, it is," he said. "All white people are racists."

By then we had reached the classroom. There was a girl in our class named Janice who was awkward and not very attractive. Most people were rude to her, and Jay was outright mean to her. I always tried to be nice to her. When we chose teams on the playground, I'd pick her as the first girl on our team. We were going to win anyway, so it was no risk for Janice to be on my team. But I was nice to her because I *wanted* to be nice to her.

As Jay and I entered the room, I walked up to Janice and said, "Which one of us is a better friend to you?"

"Wait," Jay interrupted. "That's not the question." He looked at Janice. "Who would you rather have for a best friend, Shaun or me?"

Janice's face froze. I had never seen such a stricken look on anyone's face before. Tears welled up in her eyes as she struggled to answer.

Seconds felt like minutes. Finally Jay said, "You can go ahead and tell him. It's not that big a deal. It's me, isn't it? You'd rather have me as your best friend."

Janice slowly nodded her head, agreeing with Jay. Even though Jay treated her worse than anyone in class, and I treated her better than anyone in class, she preferred to have Jay as a friend.

That moment was pivotal, and I had a choice to make. I could either hate all white people, which I could never do, or I could resolve to never allow myself to face rejection again. I chose to avoid rejection. That was a lie I accepted and an agreement I made with Satan. The lie was, "If you make yourself vulnerable in a relationship, people will reject you. They will reject you for things about yourself you can never change." That agreement formed the basis of a stronghold, one that controlled my attitudes and actions for much of my life. Addressing it and pulling down that stronghold was crucial to the effectiveness of God's ministry through me.

That's what I mean by learning about yourself. God, the Revealer of all truth, can show you things about yourself that you never realized were there. It might be a vow you made as a child: "I'll never be lazy like my father," or "I'll never be overbearing like my mother." It might be a resolution like the one I made in fifth grade. Often those words and promises are spoken in a moment of strong emotion and quickly forgotten, but they are powerful nonetheless. Those vows, rooted in anger, bitterness, and fear, have a way of connecting you to the person, event, or circumstance that hurt you. In fact, you're so connected to it that it causes you to repeat the conduct you vowed you would avoid. In my case, I wanted to avoid rejection, but I wound up rejecting others. I needed to be freed from that lie.

The Holy Spirit can lead you on a journey of reconciliation and freedom from the traps you're in.

ADD TO KNOWLEDGE...SELF-CONTROL

When you read the attributes of the fruit of the Holy Spirit, you see that after knowledge comes self-control (see 2 Peter 1:5–7). We don't hear much about self-control anymore. Most of what we hear is about instant gratification. Even with godly things, taking the quickest and most pleasurable route is usually our first choice. But the Christian life often is not quick, convenient, or easy. And the Holy Spirit's deepest work in our lives causes discomfort and sometimes pain.

The Holy Spirit's work of setting you free from the strongholds of Satan is sometimes instantaneous. However, once you are set free, you need to live differently to completely overcome a past stronghold. You need to learn new habits and attitudes so you can replace a stronghold with truth, and often that involves self-control. That path sounds simple, but it can be the most difficult walk of your life.

Self-control begins with understanding yourself, seeing your flaws and weaknesses, and taking them seriously. You have to say no to the lie you've believed in the past and yes to the truth that is being revealed to you now. Breaking free from patterns of destructive conduct begins with simply saying no. You are saying no to the lie and no to yourself, two decisions that take you to God's yes.

It can be as simple as deciding who you are going to have for friends and how much time you'll spend with them. You may have someone in your life who knows how to push you beyond the limits. The solution isn't necessarily to end that relationship but rather to decide when and how you're going to be with that person. The same thing applies to the person who lifts you up and helps you reach a higher level. Having self-control means you make the decision to be around the one who encourages you and lifts you up, and you limit your time with those who push you in the opposite direction. Self-control is really about your will and choosing to give God control over it.

The great thing about self-control is that it works whether you like it or not. When I was a kid, I saw guys graduate from high school and head off to play football in college. The next year they'd come back to our school for homecoming or to a basketball game. I was always amazed at how they had changed. Our high school coaches believed in using the weightroom, and our players always had good size. But every time one of these graduates showed up after being in college a year or two, they were *huge.* Some of them looked twice as big as when they left our town. At the time I didn't know how that happened. A few years later, when I arrived at the University of Alabama, I learned the secret.

Almost every football team has a strength-training program. If you want to play on the team, you have to go to the weightroom and follow that program. In college the guys have their own cooks, and they dictate the kinds of things you eat. Controlling both exercise and diet creates a great environment for physical growth. With good food, plenty of exercise, and some of the best strength coaches in the world, a young kid out of high school can add a lot of muscle.

Now the interesting thing about weight training is that it works whether you like it or not. Some days I went to the weightroom excited to lift weights and put in the work. Other days I went but hated every minute of it. Either way, my muscles received the exercise. As a result they became bigger and stronger.

That same thing happens with self-control. It makes no difference whether you want to drive past a bar or you want to stop for a drink. If you keep driving, you will begin to grow stronger in resisting the urge to drink. A mentor of mine once said, "Whatever you continually eat, you will crave." If you're eating steak, that's what you'll learn to crave. If it's Doritos, that's what you'll crave. That principle works in the opposite direction too. The appetite you starve eventually dies. If you start turning down harmful things, you'll eventually learn to like *not having them.* The key to spiritual growth is making yourself a slave to the things of God.

Paul told the Corinthians, "I beat my body and make it my slave so that after I have preached to others, I myself will not be disqualified for the prize" (1 Corinthians 9:27). From time to time I lead the men I disciple on what we call a 9:27 plan. We choose a physical area of our lives and beat our bodies into submission by taking something away—no soda for a month or something like that. At other times we work to build muscle in other, more spiritual areas. To do that, we might commit to get up at five in the morning for an hour of prayer and Bible study or some other spiritual exercise. Building spiritual muscle through learning self-control works whether you like it or not. You just have to do it.

ADD TO SELF-CONTROL...PERSEVERANCE

After self-control comes perseverance. We live in an age when few people want to control themselves and even fewer want to work at it, to gut through the worst to get to the best, much less to achieve God's best. Perseverance means sticking with something even when it seems at first not to be working. It means pushing through the things other people overlook, pushing through things that, at the time, seem insignificant.

Persevering doesn't mean just getting through the big stuff, either. Little things are just as important because, in the Kingdom of God, there are no little things. If God brings something to your attention, it's a big deal.

As I've mentioned, after I graduated from high school, I received an athletic scholarship to play football at the University of Alabama. The school has a long and storied football tradition. Since it began in 1892, the Crimson Tide football team has won thirteen national championships, dozens of conference championships, and hundreds of games. It was an honor and a dream to play for that team. My freshman year was amazing both on and off the field. I made some great friends, and I was successful in my classes. On the field I had a breakout game against LSU, and we followed the season with a great bowl game. Then came my sophomore year.

In my sophomore year, I got hurt for the first time. People began questioning whether I was good enough to be a starter. I even began to doubt myself. Coaches were riding me to do more, play harder, deal with the pain. On top of that, I took an incredibly hard economics course during the fall semester and didn't think I was going to pass. A voice whispered to me, *Quit. They don't care about you anyway, so why should you care?*

I asked a friend, "What do you do when you're having the worst day of your life? What about the worst month? What about when it's the whole semester?"

He said, "Look for joy. I surround myself with people who remind me of the good I have and how good God is to me. I also turn to Scripture."

I said, "What verse do you have for this?"

He said, "James, chapter one, verses two through four. 'Consider it pure joy…whenever you face trials.'"

We laughed as we talked, but that scripture and the advice he gave me was a word I still live by.

Consider it pure joy, my brothers, whenever you face trials of many kinds, because you know that the testing of your faith develops perseverance. Perseverance must finish its work so that you may be mature and complete, not lacking anything. (James 1:2–4)

When I get down and think nothing is working out right, I remind myself how good God is to me. I recount the things He is doing in my life, and I turn to Scripture. I also pay close attention to the people I allow to have access to my life.

In order to become a butterfly, a caterpillar must first be formed in a cocoon. To become a diamond, coal must be subjected to unthinkable heat and pressure; otherwise, it's just a lump of coal. God isn't overly concerned about your comfort. He's interested in your character. In fact, He embraces your discomfort as a means of changing your character. Your personal circumstances—the utility bill you can't pay, the food you don't have, the car that won't start—those things are tools in His hands to instill in you the qualities He desires. They are tools He uses to transform your character into the image of Christ.

Perseverance is one of the qualities He wants us to have. Perseverance. Endurance. Holding on until the very end. In order to win the race, you have to cross the finish line. The promise isn't for those who begin the race; it's for those who finish, for those who endure.

ADD TO PERSEVERANCE...GODLINESS

There is an orderly progression to God's redemptive work. No matter how haphazard it may seem, He is moving through your life in an orderly fashion. When you're a Wanderer or a Wonderer, He isn't immediately concerned about godliness. There are too many other things in your life that are pointing you in the wrong direction, so God waits before He addresses godliness. He comes to it after He gets you ready.

You started with faith, and from there you began to add goodness—God's goodness. Then God began to share His knowledge: knowledge about Himself, about Scripture, and about you. Your priorities are no longer about what the flesh wants. You passed that when you learned self-control and practiced perseverance.

So what does godliness look like? Godliness looks like Jesus on the cross. Many people know the basic Christian doctrine that Jesus died for our sins. Few ever think about what actually happened.

All of humanity was lost, separated from God by sin. Adam and Eve disobeyed God and allowed Satan access to a world that was intended to always be like the Garden of Eden. Only one Person could save us: God. In order to do that, He had to become one of us. He laid aside His identity as God and took on our identity as a human. Jesus Christ—fully God and fully man—was totally and completely selfless.

That's a glimpse of what it was like for God to become human. That's what it was like for Him to be Jesus. So when we take on the quality of godliness, we are becoming like Him. It means allowing Him to live through you and make His character qualities evident in you. The goal is all of Him and none of you, which means becoming totally selfless. That is the godliness that Jesus lived in His years on earth.

Most of us don't have a problem with allowing God to live through us when we think of it solely in terms of our relationship to Him. If it's just between God and us, we might bristle a little at what we read in the Bible or hear in our spirit. But it causes us no great personal discomfort. The trouble comes when we realize that selflessness is true selflessness only when it becomes our attitude toward others. That is when things get a lot tougher. Applying selflessness to our relationships with family, neighbors, co-workers, or that guy across the hall who irritates us without even trying—that is real godliness. Giving ourselves totally to someone we know is going to take advantage of us—that is selfless living.

Jesus pointed the way toward selflessness on the last night of His life on earth. That evening, after the disciples had eaten together and Judas had gone out to betray Jesus to the Sanhedrin, Jesus came with a basin of water and a towel. He took off His robe, knelt before each of the disciples, and washed their feet. Peter didn't like it and protested.

"No," said Peter, "you shall never wash my feet."

Jesus answered, "Unless I wash you, you have no part with me." (John 13:8)

Jesus wasn't giving a demonstration of the value of cleanliness or a lesson in humility. He was demonstrating selflessness as a precursor to a greater understanding of what was about to happen to Him. Notice, He took off His robe. He laid aside His position as King and Lord of the universe, just as He had laid it aside to become human. Then He knelt to serve the disciples, just as He would serve them the following day on the cross. Washing their feet was a sign of how they should treat each other and a demonstration of how they should carry out their roles as ministers of the gospel. And remember, while Jesus was doing this, Judas was out in the night, selling Him out to the Sanhedrin—and Jesus knew it.

The selflessness of Jesus is the goal. It's the quality of godliness that God is producing in your life.

ADD KINDNESS...AND LOVE

Following godliness comes brotherly kindness, and after that comes love. There we reach the completeness of who we are in Christ. God could have started with "Love your neighbor as yourself," but the doing of it isn't quite like that. Merely telling an Unbeliever or a Believer that the goal is to love your neighbor would convey information without the necessary context. Love, like everything else, must be learned. It is a decision and an action—not an emotion. Brotherly kindness is often equated with mere cordiality. Love, however, is much more, although it sometimes comes in small ways.

As an adult, I often forget about some of the tougher times of my childhood. There were times when we sat in the dark for a day or two because the electricity had been turned off. My mother kept it from seeming like a big deal, and her attitude protected us from what might otherwise have been a very trying experience. She worked hard, but there were months when we simply had no money. One of those times was the summer before I entered sixth grade. We didn't have enough money to buy a present for my birthday, and we didn't really celebrate it, either. I began thinking I was the cause of the trouble.

My family was riding home from Cincinnati when my mother noticed my mood. She looked at me and asked what was wrong. Tears formed in my eyes as I asked her, "Am I not important enough for us to celebrate my birthday?" And then my next question was, "Am I a burden on you?"

Instead of going home, we got off the highway at the next exit and went to the Florence Mall, where my mother bought me a blue bathrobe. I was the only person in our apartment with a robe. When I wondered why, she said, "Every king has a robe."

Thinking about that robe right now makes me smile. It was only a robe, but it said to me that my mother really did care and that I was valuable. With that one act, all the weight that had rested on my shoulders evaporated. She could have talked to me all night, explaining how important I was, and it would have never been as convincing as that one selfless act. It also taught me the value of action in demonstrating the words you say and the message you give. I've done my best to pass it on to others.

As my bride, Valerie, approached her twenty-ninth birthday, I began to plan how we would celebrate. We were living in Seattle at the time. A great friend and mentor, Greg Alex, operates the Matt Talbot Center, a center for drug addicts and the homeless. Valerie wanted to celebrate her birthday by doing something special for the center.

Instead of a party with friends, we flew Greg's daughter, Danielle, into Seattle. Danielle is a gourmet chef in Paris, and we asked her to prepare dinner at the Matt Talbot Center. Then we contacted businesses and other people we knew and asked them to provide gift bags. Next we sent invitations to all our friends and asked them to attend as servers or, if they couldn't make it, to send money. With the money we received, we purchased gift cards. On the evening of the celebration, we opened the doors of the center and invited the homeless in for a gourmet dinner. As people came in, we gave them gift bags and ushered them to their seats. They received books, CDs, football cards, Nike gifts, and an assortment of other items. Some of my recording-artist friends provided entertainment. Valerie and I, along with the friends who joined us for the evening, spent our time serving food and visiting with those who attended.

God had suggested the event to Valerie, and I knew we were doing God's will that evening. Still, I wondered if it made any difference. As I was thinking about that, a woman came up and told me how glad she was to be there. She'd been homeless for two weeks. A tragedy had happened that had put her out of her home, and she'd reached what she thought was the end. She wondered if anyone cared about her and questioned whether God still loved her. Just a few hours before, she'd been walking the streets, asking God to show her that He loved her. As she came around the corner, she saw a line of people waiting to get into the center. She asked what was going on, and they said, "Shaun Alexander, the football player, is having a party for his wife, and everyone is invited. Get in line. I don't think he'll mind if you attend."

She looked at me and said, "I thank you for the gifts and the dinner." And with a smile on her face, she said, "I know that God loves me."

This is the life of a Christian who is an Example, totally integrated from top to bottom by selfless love. You cannot skip this stage. Of all the stages in the process of spiritual maturity, this one is the most critical. The Example stage is where your talk becomes your walk. This is where all those things you read about as a Believer—Peter's night in the jail at Jerusalem, Paul and Silas in the jail at Philippi, Paul receiving whippings and beatings and escaping into the night—this is where all of that happens. The time you spend with Christ in this stage, enduring and persevering, is when you receive power for the stage that follows—the Teacher stage. You can't become a powerful Teacher without enduring the stage of being an Example.

Remember, God isn't looking for perfection. He's looking for order, His order. This part, the part of becoming an Example, of learning to live what you believe, is the most crucial part of all.

CHAPTER 9

Trials, Traps, and Victories

Everyone should be quick to listen,
slow to speak.

—JAMES (JAMES 1:19)

O f all the stages we walk through toward spiritual maturity, none is more important than that of the Example. Here, Christians learn to live what they believe. People are crying out for authenticity, and nothing answers that cry like the experience of watching someone actually live what they claim to believe. However, like every other stage of God's work in your life, this one has its own trials, traps, and victories.

THE TRIALS OF AN EXAMPLE

The most common trial confronting the Example is pride in the form of self-righteousness. Entire church denominations base their identity on outward symbols of a Christian's commitment to God. They put far too much emphasis on things such as what clothing a Christian should wear, how much makeup women are allowed to use, whether it's right to wear jewelry. Such rules are nothing more than the expectations of humans that are elevated to the authority of God's commands. This presents a serious trial for Examples, both as something to endure from others and something to avoid in their own lives.

When you commit your life to being an Example and you see yourself making some progress, it's hard not to feel proud of it. Often self-righteousness appears under circumstances that make such an attitude seem justified. You are walking as an Example for God when you notice someone who professes loyalty to Jesus deliberately doing things that go against God's will. Your first thought might easily be to respond to them with condemnation. "How could you do that? What were you thinking? Can't you see that what you're doing is wrong?"

Making ourselves the judge of others is simply substituting our judgment for God's. The Example's role is not to make those decisions for other Christians. An Example's role is to represent Christ to the world. Jesus never told anyone what to wear, and He never definitively answered doctrinal questions. On the contrary, He concentrated on building relationships with a great variety of people. He ate with sinners and hung out with outcasts, while avoiding religious arguments.

The religious leaders of Jesus' day lived within a small box. They limited the type of people with whom they would associate, maintaining relationships only with those who met their criteria of how God's people should live. They did their best to impose that same tight standard on everyone they met. They even put God in a box, limiting what they expected Him to do. And when they encountered Jesus, they tried to put Him in the same box.

Jesus had many opportunities to follow the lead of the Pharisees and Sadducees. He could have limited the circle of those whom He chose to associate with. He could have brought judgment on people who, outwardly, seemed to deserve His wrath. The woman caught in adultery comes to mind. Yet He never once told that woman how bad she was. He just asked the question: "Has no one condemned you?" (John 8:10).

Jesus was still standing there after the other men had dropped their stones and walked away. He could have issued a condemnation, but He didn't. I think He asked the woman that question with the kindest smile imaginable.

The trial that confronts Examples today is the same one Jesus faced: to avoid self-righteousness, to step outside the box, and to devote attention, time, and energy to loving others into the Kingdom of God. People can be changed forever simply by what happens when they meet an Example. Your life can draw Unbelievers to Jesus. But to do that you'll sometimes have to go to places that other Christians think you should never visit. You might have to endure their disapproval, but you'll have the opportunity to join God in doing things that only He would do.

Jesus was not interested in arguments about religious doctrine. Instead, He concentrated on dining with sinners, spending time with tax collectors, and avoiding the external trappings of religion.

THE TRAPS OF AN EXAMPLE

There are two traps for Examples. One is the sense that they have to be perfect. As I mentioned earlier, Jesus isn't looking for perfection. He's looking for devotion and order.

I've been blessed to watch hundreds of young men grow up through the five stages of spiritual maturity. They began as Unbelievers, became Believers through faith in Christ, then grew to become Examples and beyond. In their lives one of the deadliest traps I've seen is the trap of thinking they have to be perfect. One who had a real struggle with this is a guy I'll call Johnny.

Johnny was a great Example to his friends and co-workers. He loved Jesus and was all about loving people and exhorting them into the Kingdom. He and I met together regularly for Bible study, prayer, and accountability. On each of those occasions, I asked him about life and girls and alcohol—my usual questions. Each time I asked, he would say, "I'm doing great. God is good."

Then one day I realized that Johnny never had a bad day. That's when I knew he was falling for the perfection trap. I arranged a time to meet him, and when we got together, I told him, "I need to apologize."

He looked puzzled. "What for?"

"I think you need to know how flawed I am. I mess up daily. I'm not good enough to be in the army of Christ. But God's grace is so good, He'll take a little mess-up like me and still use me."

A tear rolled down Johnny's cheek. He said, "I've been drinking, and nobody knows it."

I hugged him and said, "It's Satan that says you have to be perfect. But God says something different. He says you have to be obedient."

As we talked, Johnny told me that once he gave in to drinking, he felt ashamed, so he didn't tell anyone. "I couldn't tell you. You look at me different."

I told him, "I've never looked for you to be perfect. I don't look for any Christian to be flawless. We all have fallen at one time or another."

Johnny then began to explain the spiritual beating he had received from Satan. After he started drinking, he felt like a failure, which led him to believe he was a liar, which led him to believe he was a hypocrite. How could he be a Christian and an Example and be drinking like that? Over time, the lies of Satan led Johnny to think he wasn't really saved.

In a short time he had gotten involved with drugs, girls, parties—all the things that appeal to the flesh. It happened, not because he was curious, but because he'd fallen into the trap of expecting perfection. Perfection is a goal you can't attain in this life. Once it becomes your goal and you don't reach it, you think you can never reach it, and you give up. That's all Satan wants, so he can defeat you.

Johnny had to repent and recommit his life and ways to Jesus, which he did. The trap he had fallen into left major scars, still visible a year later. This experience taught both of us a valuable lesson: Christians don't have to be perfect. The mind-set that you have to look a certain way in somebody else's eyes is the setup for a perfect trap of Satan's.

The second trap Examples face is thinking they have grown so much, come so far, and gone so deep that they no longer need regular time alone with God. Examples can start to think they no longer need to spend regular time studying Scripture and praying. Falling into that trap can lead to disaster.

The model prayer Jesus gave His disciples—what we call the Lord's Prayer—contains a line that says, "Give us today our daily bread" (Matthew 6:11). In Jesus' day, people did not have many ways of preserving food. Most of what they ate was consumed on the same day it was prepared. Workers were paid at the end of the day so they could buy what they needed for the evening meal. That's why they prayed for daily bread. We still pray that way, but we don't always have a full understanding of the meaning.

I was teaching the Lord's Prayer to my little girls one day. They asked, "Shouldn't we pray for daily bread every day?"

I told them, "God said, 'I give each one what they need for that day, so always focus on the day.'"

This day is all we have, and God wants us focused on overcoming the trials and traps of each day and gaining the victories of each day. Living in the past or living in the future is a dangerous practice. God wants us living with Him in the present, so He gives us only what we need for each day's challenges. That includes what we need physically, mentally, emotionally, and spiritually.

Mental bread is knowledge, wisdom, and insight for the things you're going to face. Physical bread is the bread that makes you healthy and whole. It gives you strength to do the tasks for that day. Emotional bread keeps you in tune with the feelings of the people around you. It's not good to overreact, to read too much into your circumstances or the reactions people have to you. Wisdom and insight work along with your emotions to help keep you level, not too high and not too low. Remember, God works through order and not chaos.

Spiritual bread is the daily presence of the Holy Spirit. It is God living in you and on you and you sensing how to do what God wants you to do. The trap facing an Example is this: Satan will do whatever he can to get you to believe you are walking so strong that you don't need the daily bread from God. Satan's traps for Examples are deadly. They aren't designed just to make you fall. They are there to bring you down and keep you down and to bring others down with you. You can never grow so far spiritually that you don't need Jesus daily.

THE VICTORIES OF AN EXAMPLE

As I prayed about the five stages of spiritual maturity and as God developed those concepts in my mind, I looked back through my life and the lives of the Christians who have taught and led me. One thing I noticed is that the Example has the greatest influence on Unbelievers, the Wanderers and the Wonderers. If you ask people what brought them to believe Jesus was real, the first thing most of them will say is, "I saw someone do this, or I remember watching someone do that." Most of the time, the person they were watching was someone who had reached the Example stage. How those Examples lived opened the Unbelievers' minds to the possibility that Jesus really lives.

When I first became a Believer, I couldn't really explain what was happening to me, but I knew I was different. My best friend was excited for me, but the changes in my life and what I was experiencing had no effect on him.

Ten years later I was an Example. My friend saw me then and said, "I've watched you love me when I shouldn't have been treated so well. I've seen how different you are from the rest of us. I want what you have. I believe in your God." The first victory for Examples is when, without even opening their mouths, they by their influence help turn Wanderers and Wonderers into Believers.

The next stage of spiritual maturity for Examples is to become Teachers. Stepping into that stage opens up an entirely new area of ministry. As you move through the Example stage, you begin to get a taste of what's to come as a Teacher.

CHAPTER 10

Peter as an Example

Imagine me being free,
trusting you totally.
Finally, I can.
—KIRK FRANKLIN, "IMAGINE ME"

By the time Jesus was crucified, Peter had moved into the Example stage. He had heard Jesus' call to follow Him, and he followed. As a Believer, he had heard Jesus teach, and he had seen Jesus perform miracles. When Jesus sent the disciples out to do ministry on their own, Peter had experienced the joy of seeing Jesus' words and presence become real in his own life.

But Peter was an impulsive guy, speaking or acting first and figuring things out later. He hadn't yet developed a well-rounded character, and God hadn't finished dealing with him on many of the major issues in his life. Still, he was living out of a desire and a commitment to love God. Peter was a passionate follower of Christ, but a potentially fatal trap awaited him.

On the night Jesus was arrested, Peter followed the guards as they took Jesus back to the high priest and then to the Sanhedrin. He tagged along, watching to see what would happen. While he waited in the courtyard, a young woman noticed him and pointed him out to the others as one of Jesus' disciples. That is when Peter fell victim to one of the traps of the Example stage.

Earlier that evening, while Jesus prayed, Peter had slept. Jesus came to him to warn him, and He even awakened him to alert him to the trap. But Peter fell back asleep. By the time Peter awakened once again, the trap had been sprung. Jesus knew what was going to happen that night, and He knew Peter needed to pray. That's why He came back to warn him. He had even warned Peter earlier that, when the time came, Peter would deny he ever knew Jesus (see Mark 14:27–31; Matthew 26:31–35). Yet Peter did nothing to guard against that day.

As unbelievable as it sounds, Peter, who had seen his own mother-in-law healed at Jesus' hands (see Mark 1:29–31), children healed (see John 4:43–54), demons cast out (see Mark 1:21–28), and the dead brought back to life (see John 11:1–44), denied that he ever knew Jesus. He had seen Jesus heal the sick close up. (A woman in the crowd touched the hem of Jesus' robe and was healed; see Luke 8:43–48.) And Peter had seen Jesus heal from far away. (A ruler of the synagogue asked Jesus to heal his daughter who was near death. Word soon came that the girl had died, and Jesus spoke words of faith and healing on the way to the man's home; see Mark 5:21–24, 35–43.)

Peter had witnessed miracles that only Jesus' closest disciples had seen. But even so, shortly after Jesus was arrested, when He could have used a strong witness, Peter lied and said he'd never known Him.

That's the trap of the Example, demonstrated by Peter's falling asleep in the garden. Examples can be trapped into believing the lie that they have grown so far they no longer need to pray or study the Scriptures. They can be trapped by the lie that they don't need to keep getting stronger in their faith, that they no longer need to prepare for the next battle with the enemy. No matter how much you grow spiritually, you are never too mature to be above Satan's deception. You will never become so mature that you don't have to constantly watch, fight, and pray.

After the resurrection Jesus restored Peter to fellowship with Him and with the other disciples. Peter went on to become a leader in the early church. In restoring Peter to his position, Jesus instilled in him an assurance of three things—each one crucial to Peter's continued growth, to his future ministry, and to the life of the church. If you are to continue growing as an Example, you will need to know these three things as well.

1. You need to know who you are.
2. You need to know whose you are.
3. You need to know your assignment.

KNOW WHO YOU ARE AND WHOSE YOU ARE

When I was a kid playing in the PeeWee Football League, there was a team called the Black Hawks. It wasn't the team I played for, but sometimes I wished it were. They brought a large group of parents with them to every game. Before and after the game, regardless of whether they won or lost, the parents sang this cheer: "We are the Black Hawks, mighty, mighty Black Hawks. Everywhere we go, people want to know who we are, so we tell them." And then it started over. They won a lot of games, but the thing that attracted me was they had an identity and they knew it.

A preacher once told about a pastor who was walking down a hall in his church. The music minister greeted him with a smile. "I gave your son a dollar for the candy bar he wanted."

"Thanks," the pastor said.

The pastor continued down the hallway and soon reached the classroom door of his son's favorite teacher. The teacher stopped class. "Your son was in the last class. Not this one." Then she leaned over. "And I gave him a dollar," she whispered.

As the bell for lunch rang, the pastor went to his office, and there was his son, sitting behind the desk.

"Hey, Dad," he said with candy all over his face.

"Son," the pastor began, "don't make this a habit, going around asking for money. You know they wouldn't be so nice if we didn't have the same last name."

The son nodded and took a drink of soda. As he swallowed, he looked up at his father. "But, Dad," he said with a grin, "we do have the same last name."

The son knew who he was and whose he was. To be an Example, you must know who you are exemplifying. You must know who you are in Christ and who died to purchase your salvation.

Jesus posed this question to His disciples. As they were traveling to Caesarea Philippi, He asked them what people were saying about Him and who they thought He was. The disciples told Him what they'd heard. Some thought Jesus was John the Baptist come back from the dead. Others thought He was Elijah or another of the prophets.

> "But what about you?" he [Jesus] asked. "Who do you say I am?"
> Peter answered, "You are the Christ." (Mark 8:29)

Peter knew who Jesus was. That one answer also told Peter who he was. It gave Peter a vision and an identity.

KNOW YOUR ASSIGNMENT

Once you know who you are and whom you are serving, you need to know your assignment. I have great respect for privates in the army. They are the lowest rank in the entire organization. They usually are assigned the jobs that are the hardest and that get the least recognition. In baseball, a similar role would be a middle reliever. He's a pitcher who comes in for only an inning or two at most. He is not expected to stay in the game to finish it and win it. Fans remember the pitcher who started the game and the closer who pulled out a victory. The middle reliever never gets credited with a save, and only the most ardent fans remember the guy who took the mound in the middle of the game.

On the football field, the unsung player is the fullback. His job is to throw his body in front of oncoming tacklers and protect the running back. He rarely carries the ball, and when he does, it's usually straight ahead for short yardage against impossible odds. He's often the ballcarrier you see running headlong into a wall of defensive linemen.

If you talked to the private in the army, the middle reliever in baseball, or the fullback on a football field, each would say the same thing. "I have a job to do, and I do it." Perks and attention are great, but all they really need is a tough assignment, and they go out there and get it done.

Knowing your assignment focuses your attention on how to get the task done, and it helps you think through the sacrifices you will have to make to accomplish it. Jesus said, "If anyone would come after me, he must deny himself and take up his cross and follow me" (Mark 8:34). Completing your assignment requires that same kind of commitment.

Peter received his assignment from Jesus, which was, "Follow Me." His job was to walk with Jesus. The night after Jesus was arrested, Peter understood all too clearly that completing his assignment meant carrying his own cross. Even though he gave in to fear and shrank from that assignment for a moment, he came back later to accept the challenge. After Pentecost, Peter was all-in for whatever Jesus wanted him to do. You must be all-in too.

Thinking of that reminds me of my friend Ken. Several of us wanted to play golf one day, so a friend started rounding up players. Ken was one of the guys he called. Ken had never played golf before, but he agreed to join us. When I heard he was going to play, I was amused. "This ought to be fun," I said. Ken was so competitive and intense about every challenge; I knew the game would be interesting.

As planned, we arrived at the golf course and walked out to the first tee. Everyone else teed off, then Ken placed his ball in the tee box. He drew back his club and swung. *Ping!* Just by the sound of it, we knew he'd hit a solid shot.

"Wow, you killed it!" someone exclaimed.

"Man, I didn't know you played golf."

"I don't," Ken said with a grin. "But after you invited me to join you, I had an instructor teach me when and how to use every club and every swing. I became a student of the game."

Ken still plays golf. He has remained a student of the game. If we were playing now, Ken would be asking questions about the clubs we were using, the course layout, which way the grass was growing, and everything else he needed to know so he could succeed.

When an Example is all-in, he does the same thing. He becomes a student of the things of God, always growing, always learning, always hungry for more, no matter what it takes. As we do that, Christ's character continues to grow in us, taking us to new levels of maturity and understanding and, with them, new insight and new ministry.

As Pentecost arrived, Peter knew for certain what his role would be among the disciples. He knew he was a major leader of the first followers of Jesus. He was an apostle of Christ, a witness to the life and resurrection of Jesus. He knew who he was. Peter also knew whose he was. He was a man devoted solely to Jesus. And he knew his assignment—to go into all the land teaching and making disciples. He was committed to the completion of that assignment and ultimately gave his life for it.

As an Example, Peter was all-in.

PART 4

The Teacher

Now the overseer must be above reproach,
the husband of but one wife, temperate,
self-controlled, respectable, hospitable,
able to teach, not given to drunkenness,
not violent but gentle, not quarrelsome, not
a lover of money.

—PAUL, THE APOSTLE (1 TIMOTHY 3:2–3)

Even though you have ten thousand
guardians in Christ, you do not have
many fathers.

—PAUL, THE APOSTLE (1 CORINTHIANS 4:15)

CHAPTER 11

Becoming a Teacher

> Therefore let us leave the elementary teachings about Christ and go on to maturity, not laying again the foundation of repentance from acts that lead to death, and of faith in God, instruction about baptisms, the laying on of hands, the resurrection of the dead, and eternal judgment.
>
> —HEBREWS 6:1–2

When it is conveyed in the proper context, information can transform individuals and even society. It can change people and relationships. It can redirect personal behavior and the way entire communities function. But without the right motivation, information is useless. The motivation to do something with the information you receive comes from the context in which the information is taught. That's why those who work in education will tell you that context is everything to the learning process.

The fourth stage of God's work in your life is to develop you as a Teacher. A Teacher is the coach, the mentor, the helper, the trainer, the educator. He or she helps you develop and keeps you motivated, giving you the background and the foundation you need to take your life and faith to the next level. A conversation I had with Richard, one of the men I disciple, is a good illustration of this.

One day Richard asked me a question about life. It was one of those "which thing is better" questions. I didn't answer him directly. Instead, I asked him a question.

"Richard, what do you think is better: to do a godly thing or to do God's thing?"

Godly things are good, but when you do God's thing, it's even better. When you do God's thing, you are doing a godly thing the way God wants it done at the time God wants it done. We all need to learn how to hear from God and be obedient to His voice. That's because doing something that appears godly—but doing it at the wrong time—can make it ungodly. A Teacher will help you learn how to do God's thing, in God's way, at God's time. The Teacher helps mold and shape a person into the image of Christ.

When I think of Teachers, I think of the American Missionary Movement (AMM) and the schools they established in the American South after the Civil War. Teachers at those schools came from the Northeast, where they had been steeped in classic liberalism—the idea that humanity could improve through human effort. They believed people could work and do the right things and one day rise above human circumstances and usher in the perfect society. That philosophy proved inadequate, but it formed the context for the education of many African Americans during the first half of the twentieth century.

In the AMM schools, education did not consist of simply providing students with information. Instead, information was conveyed in the context of the black experience in America for the purpose of transforming life in America. Those schools produced men and women such as Dr. Martin Luther King Jr., Coretta Scott King, Edythe Scott Bagley, and many others who went on to lead the civil rights movement. Bare information is only information, but information that is taught in context is empowering. The AMM schools made the context clear: we can band together to build a better society. And it empowered African American leaders to make dramatic, sweeping changes in American life. That empowerment was made possible by Teachers.

Scripture provides an interesting context in its use of the word *teacher.* Paul uses the word in a technical sense to describe an office or gift. For example, in his first letter to the Corinthians, he differentiates between apostle, prophet, and teacher (see 1 Corinthians 12:28). In his letter to the Ephesians, he draws a distinction between apostles, prophets, evangelists, pastors, and teachers (see Ephesians 4:11). All are called to teach others in the sense of making disciples and conveying the Christian faith to the next generation (see Matthew 28:19–20). Some Christians are given that task as a position and office in the church. When that is done, it comes about as a special manifestation of the Holy Spirit's power. When you have not been made a Teacher in terms of position and office, you do it as part of your personal walk with Christ and the general obligation of all Christians to make disciples.

In the gospel of John, Jesus goes a step further and adopts the title of Teacher for Himself. He talked about it while He washed the disciples' feet, and He commanded them to follow His example. "You call me 'Teacher' and 'Lord,' and rightly so, for that is what I am. Now that I, your Lord and Teacher, have washed your feet, you also should wash one another's feet" (John 13:13–14).

From that context we learn that *teacher* and *servant* are synonymous. You can't just provide disciples with information; you have to invest yourself in them. This is why the Example stage precedes that of Teacher. Completing the Example stage takes you to a heightened sense of selflessness. Separated from your own priorities, you are free to allow God to use you in any way possible, including washing someone's feet. But Jesus didn't stop there; He took His commitment as Teacher to His disciples much further.

In that same gospel, Jesus refers to Himself as the Good Shepherd.

> I am the good shepherd. The good shepherd lays down his life for the sheep. The hired hand is not the shepherd who owns the sheep. So when he sees the wolf coming, he abandons the sheep and runs away. Then the wolf attacks the flock and scatters it. The man runs away because he is a hired hand and cares nothing for the sheep. (John 10:11–13)

Jesus not only took on the role of servant; He put Himself in harm's way for the sake of the people He'd been called to lead. He defined Himself as Teacher by taking on the role of servant and good shepherd.

By contrast, in the Synoptic Gospels—Matthew, Mark, and Luke—Jesus tells the disciples not to call each other *teacher.* "Nor are you to be called 'teacher,' for you have one Teacher, the Christ" (Matthew 23:10). Once again, context is everything.

TEACHERS AS SERVANTS AND SHEPHERDS

In the Synoptic Gospels, Jesus was constantly challenged by the Pharisees and the scribes over legal issues pertaining to the interpretation of Jewish law. They peppered Him with theoretical and hypothetical questions to see if He would answer "correctly" (by their standards). They were not genuinely interested in finding answers to pressing personal issues but wanted only to test Jesus and to show His supposed lack of authority as a Teacher. When Jesus told His disciples not to be teachers, He meant that the disciples should not act like the rabbis, teachers, and religious authorities of their day. He always said, "Be like me," and being like Jesus means being a Teacher within the servant–good shepherd context.

Jesus was all-in for His guys. He was all-in for each of us, even to the point of death. Teachers might not be called upon to die for someone else, but they will be called upon to step outside their comfort zone, to set aside their own desires, preferences, and goals for the good of those they are leading.

When I was growing up in Florence, Kentucky, I lived next to a horse park. The city of Lexington, less than an hour south of Florence, has some of the most beautiful countryside in the nation, much of it covered with acres of horse pasture. Horses are a big part of the economy and lifestyle in that region.

One of my favorite horse movies is *Seabiscuit,* a story about a racehorse that was famous during the 1930s and 1940s. As the story begins, Seabiscuit is lazy and lethargic. As a result he is sold at a bargain price. A trainer with a keen eye for talent then finds a way to get the best out of the horse on the racetrack.

At the same time, Seabiscuit's owner meets a jockey who is in similar shape to the horse. Horse and rider eventually get together and win lots of races. Then, late in the horse's career, both horse and jockey are injured. As they help each other rehab, events propel them toward one final race, and this is my favorite part of the movie.

Seabiscuit was a finisher. He would open slow and hang with the field, then win a race with a burst of speed near the end. The horse could outrun anything on the track, as long as he sensed a challenge. He needed to be pushed to be his best. Otherwise, he loafed.

In the final race, Seabiscuit became separated from the field. As he lagged behind the other horses, he became lethargic. Then an amazing thing happened. One of the other jockeys, a friend of the guy riding

Seabiscuit, dropped his horse back and ran alongside Seabiscuit. That meant his horse would never win the race. But Seabiscuit was spurred on by the competition and immediately started running flat out. He caught the field and blew past them to win by four lengths.

This scene is a perfect example of the selfless Teacher—a servant and a shepherd. Jesus was God in the flesh. He laid aside His place in heaven and took on human flesh so He could drop back and pick you up. Because you are a Teacher, and as a Teacher you are a servant and shepherd, Jesus calls you to do the same for those around you.

TEACHERS CHANGE LIVES

Some of the most influential teachers in my life weren't teachers in the sense we're using the term in this book, but they displayed the same qualities. One of those was Mrs. Walton, my sixth-grade science teacher. All my brothers are brilliant and have done well in life. Durran earned an academic scholarship to Notre Dame and played in the marching band. Donte is a computer engineer, and Ronnie is a training sergeant in the U.S. Army. Tony excels at being Tony.

When I reached the sixth grade, I was assigned to Mrs. Walton's science class. She had taught Durran the year before and was excited to have me as a student. Durran was one of the smartest kids in his class. He knew the answer to every question and was the kind of student every teacher longs to teach. I wasn't quite like that. In the sixth grade I was already known for my athletic ability, but I was determined to be more than just a good athlete. I decided I was going to work hard and be better than Durran in the classroom.

Early in that year we had a science test. To say I did poorly on it would be an understatement. I bombed the thing. When we got our tests back, I saw I had received a failing grade. Mrs. Walton talked to me about it after class. Standing there in front of her, I was reduced to tears. She wanted to know what was wrong and why I was so upset.

"You just want me to be like Durran," I stammered.

A look of concern came over her. "What are you talking about?"

"He's smart and gets everything right, and you just want me to be like him."

"Shaun," she replied, "you don't have to be like your brother. You just need to be the best Shaun Alexander the world has ever seen." She smiled and continued, "When you're done being that guy, the whole world will stand up and applaud him."

Those were powerful words. At the sound of them, a heavy weight rolled off my back, and I was free. I didn't have to measure up to Durran. I was Shaun, created for a special purpose, a purpose no one else could fulfill. Those words of liberation didn't come from a sermon on Sunday or a friend in the hallway. They came from a teacher.

In the twelfth grade I had a calculus teacher named Mr. Vanover. I was a senior playing football and working hard to graduate. By then, colleges were recruiting me, and ESPN had reporters following me around. It was fun, but it made for a hectic year. One weekend that fall I played in a football game on Friday night, then drove up to Michigan for a recruiting visit during the Colorado-Michigan football game. It was an exciting weekend, with the game and all the activities they use to get high school athletes interested in their university.

I came home after the game and went to church on Sunday. I knew I had a calculus test the next day, but I was certain I knew the information and figured I would do well. That next day as I sat in class and stared at the test paper, I was stumped. I confused one formula with another, and nothing made any sense. I kept telling myself, *This is your subject.* But I just couldn't work the problems. I did my best, but I knew the grade wasn't going to be good. So when I finished, I wrote a note on the answer sheet.

"Dear Mr. Vanover. I was at the Colorado-Michigan game this weekend. I know this stuff, but it is not making any sense to me today. I promise you that this will be the worst test I will score for you ever."

Mr. Vanover talked to me afterward. I didn't know what he would say. He was always really cool with us and very much aware of the challenges we faced as students, but he also believed students should put in the work the class required. I would not have been surprised to hear a speech about "You have to work harder and not play around so much. You don't have time to waste." But he didn't do that.

Instead, he smiled and said, "I appreciate your honesty. Life has choices. You made choices and owned up to the results. You didn't try to make excuses. This is good."

On the next calculus test, I made an A. Mr. Vanover wrote on it: "Shaun, I was going to grade the test on a curve to increase everyone's scores, but you busted the curve. Congratulations. Thank you for keeping your word."

At the University of Alabama, Dr. Dulek gave us a take-home test. We were supposed to study for the test, then take it on our own in the library. All of us were obligated by the student honor code not to cheat. I spent half a day getting ready for it, then went over to the library to take the test. When I saw the test questions, I knew I was in trouble. I only recognized half the problems on it. As you can imagine, I flunked it.

Dr. Dulek called me to his office and asked what had happened. All I could say was, "I guess you can tell I didn't cheat."

As a result of failing that test, I had to make an A on the final exam to get a B for the class. If I made a C or lower on the test, I wouldn't graduate. I studied hard and did my best, but I wasn't sure I had scored high enough. A few days later I went to Dr. Dulek's office to get the news. As I waited to see him, one of the other professors told me, "Dulek's been talking about you all morning."

I thought, *Oh no. I failed.*

Dr. Dulek was seated at his desk when I walked into his office. He had a wry smile on his face. "I've been telling people about you all day."

"Yes sir. I heard."

"Shaun, your test was one of the best in the class. Congratulations. You made an A."

Years later another Alabama graduate told me that story. I asked him how he knew about the incident. He told me Dr. Dulek used me as an example of what not to do with the take-home test and what to do for the final.

TEACH FROM YOUR LIFE

Teachers don't just give you information. They give you the benefit of the things they've seen and heard and done and experienced. To be a great Teacher, you have to live the life of an Example. Living the walk gives power to your talk.

My father left us when I was a young boy. Mother raised my brother Durran and me by herself in Shenandoah Apartments. When I was eleven years old, my grandmother, my father's mother, died. None of my brothers attended her funeral. Donte was working. Ronnie and Tony were in the army overseas. Durran was at band camp. I was the only one of the boys who was there.

When my father saw that I was the only one of his sons to attend his mother's funeral, he thought about his father's funeral. None of his brothers or sisters was close enough to their father to care about even handling the funeral arrangements. That thought shook up my father. He realized he didn't have a meaningful connection with any of us kids. As a result, he started to spend time with me. He called often, came to most of my games, and never missed a birthday or holiday.

For a long time I thought I received all that attention only because I was a good athlete. I wanted to know if that was the reason, so one day I asked him. He told me about the funeral and seeing me and how it made him feel like he had failed with his other sons, and he didn't want to fail with me. His attention had a powerful effect on my life, and although he did not come to know the Lord until later, his efforts to step into the role of father was one of the reasons I developed confidence in myself as a man.

Words have power. When we speak them, that power is released. My father called me Champ more than he called me Shaun or Son. His words became part of my identity. I was a champion. My father, a Teacher, told me so.

Teachers become fathers and mothers to those they are discipling. They feel the blows of their students' experiences. When the students cry, the Teachers cry. When the students win, the Teachers win. Teachers are there for the ups and downs, successes and failures.

The church is supposed to be a hospital, led by a great Doctor. Church members, being doctors themselves, are to be like fathers and mothers who care for the sick and dying. Instead, some churches have become country clubs led by motivational speakers who are trying to sell spiritual trinkets and get donations. But great Teachers become great doctors who heal the sick and dying. Great Teachers are great physical therapists who train and restore those who need to learn how to walk or how to walk again.

As a Teacher, you must remain diligent. The church needs you desperately.

CHAPTER 12

Trials, Traps, and Victories

It only takes a little dirt to make mud.
—BEN BROWN

Paul told Timothy, "If anyone sets his heart on being an overseer,[1] he desires a noble task" (1 Timothy 3:1). That statement very much applies to a Teacher, as I am using the term in this book. A Teacher is not one who simply educates but one who does so from the power of his life, from the power of having learned to be an Example. As you move on from concentrating primarily on your walk to focus on helping others with theirs, the enemy will oppose you with special trials and traps, but the victory that awaits you and those who follow you makes it all worthwhile.

THE TRIALS OF A TEACHER

The challenge facing a Teacher is that of teaching while remaining a servant. Because of the influence they have over their students, Teachers often are tempted to adopt an exaggerated sense of their own importance. This usually shows itself in a Teacher's reluctance to let go of a student. Sometimes a Teacher might feel the student is rebelling when the frustrated student no longer submits himself to the Teacher's leadership.

At the University of Alabama we had a coach named Ivy Williams. Even now when I think of Coach Williams, I tense up. He was the coach who recruited me and was one of the big reasons I went to Alabama. His bluntness and focus were tough—real tough—and difficult to endure. All my life I had been told how great I was and how special I was and how much talent I had. Coach Williams could not have cared less. The discipline he imposed on me and the manner in which he did it were quite different from what I had experienced before. I learned to develop a thick skin.

During my freshman year, we were preparing to play Auburn in the biggest game of the year. Unless you've lived in Alabama or attended the Alabama-Auburn game, it's difficult to imagine how a college game could be such a big event. For a typical Saturday college game, fans show up on Friday, have a loud night, and tailgate in the stadium parking lot on Saturday morning. But when Alabama plays Auburn, fans start showing up on *Wednesday* with campers and motor homes. The number of people on campus triples or quadruples.

The week before that game my freshman year, the coaches worked us hard and drove us relentlessly. We would run a play that seemed to work perfectly, but then they'd have us do it again and again. All the time they were yelling at us about things that seemed almost insignificant.

At one of those practices, Coach Williams barked at me, then turned to one of the other running backs who had made a mistake and yelled, "Hey, son, what's your major?"

"Marine biology," the guy replied.

Coach Williams, who always had a response, gave him a look of disgust and scoffed, "You do it like that, you're gonna drown."

He was always tough on us, but that week he was really rough.

On Saturday the stadium was packed. The band was playing. People were yelling and screaming on every play. My family was there, watching the game. I played a little, which was a great honor for a freshman, and I did well. We won the game, scoring a touchdown on the final drive to win by one point, 24–23. It was a huge game for me, and I was living the dream. But still Ivy Williams would not let up.

During my sophomore year, he was even tougher. I felt like I was one of his favorites, but at every practice he found a way to rip into all of us. I can still hear his voice shouting at me, "You will get better, or you will quit!"

In my junior year, the same thing happened, only by then I was a starter. Coach Williams's rhetoric changed from driving to challenging. "You want to be the man? We'll see." Then with a wisp of a sinister smile, he would say, "We're gonna see what you've got indeed." That year, I was an all-SEC player and could have left college early for the NFL. Instead, I decided to return for my senior year.

When I came back for practice my senior year, I prepared to face Coach Williams one last time. I was a Heisman Trophy front-runner and popular on campus. But I knew I had to humble myself to Coach Williams and continue to grow as a football player. I was certain he'd ride me from July to December, and if we made it to a bowl game, he'd be on me until New Year's Day. Much to my delight, that all changed.

One day I had to go to his office to discuss something about an upcoming game. As I started up the stairs, I could hear him talking on the telephone. His voice was loud and animated. When I got near his office door, I overheard him say, "Let me tell you something. This is his year. He's ready. And he is going to dominate the offensive side of the ball." A tingle ran up my spine. I knew he was talking about me, and I loved it. When he hung up the phone, I walked into his office.

We spent a few minutes talking about the game and the team, then I turned to leave. He said with a smile, "Shaun, I won't have to ride you like I used to."

I grinned and said, "Coach Williams, I heard what you said on the phone, and I'm going to make you right."

Coach Williams knew how to motivate guys to play football. He was a master at driving us to the breaking point. He could turn the best day into the worst in a matter of minutes. But when the time came to turn us loose, he didn't try to hold us back. He said some harsh things to me and to others on the team, but after my freshman year I never doubted for one minute that he had my best interests at heart.

That's the role of a Teacher. Instruct, push, prod, coax, and drive, but always with the best interest of the pupil at heart. And when the time comes for the students to step out on their own, you let them go. A Teacher is essential to the process of redemption. The Kingdom of God advances because of the work of those who instruct the next generation, but the Teacher is no more important than the pupil.

Teach from your life

Enduring the trials that confront a Teacher and remaining within the servant model also means limiting your teaching to the kinds of things you have experienced and lived. That doesn't mean you shouldn't speak about what God has revealed to you in Scripture. Teachers should always address the full range of issues and topics covered in Scripture. Otherwise, they run the risk of passing on theology that reflects only their personal experience and not God's self-revelation. However, a Teacher who attempts to teach without reference to his own experience also runs a big risk. He can deceive himself by thinking that, because he has taught on a topic, he has allowed God to search his heart on that topic too. Those two — teaching on a topic and allowing God to deal with you personally on a topic — are separate and very different experiences.

Teaching on a topic is simply imparting information. But teaching about an issue while wrestling with that issue on a personal level adds context and turns the information into a powerful, transforming tool. With it, the Holy Spirit's work in your life and in the student's life becomes a dynamic, vibrant experience. Without it, Teachers are merely putting themselves on a pedestal.

Fred Price Jr. faced this issue when he assumed responsibility for ministry at Crenshaw Christian Center,[2] a large Los Angeles church founded by his father. Fred Price Sr. preached around the world, wrote books on a wide range of topics, and appeared regularly on television. Following in his footsteps was a tall order, one filled with plenty of chances for missteps. A guy stepping into that position could easily be tempted to have an inflated opinion of himself and attempt to duplicate the style and content of his predecessor.

When the board asked Fred Jr. about the kind of ministry he would have and whether he would teach and preach on the topics his father addressed, he told them, "I won't preach about anything I haven't lived myself. I can only preach about what I've lived through. What I totally know that I know. There are some things I'm still going through. I won't teach that until God walks me through it and releases me."

Walking through the subject matter with your students takes this approach one step further and places the Teacher in the servant–good shepherd model. Doing that might appear risky, placing the Teacher in a vulnerable position, but that is the approach Jesus took and the life to which we are called. After all, it is not our truth we are conveying and modeling, but God's. He humbled Himself and took the risk of being vulnerable, even to the point of death. Our effectiveness as Teachers rests on our ability to take that same risk.

THE TRAPS OF A TEACHER

Once you become a Believer, there is always the trap of thinking you've come far enough that you don't need to keep studying. That is the trap of the Example, and it is a trap the Teacher faces too. If you are conscientious and intentional about how you mentor your group, avoiding that trap will be much easier. Constantly preparing new material for those you are discipling keeps you on your knees and in the Scriptures. But you have to do more than just prepare for teaching your disciples. Doing only that robs you of a dynamic personal relationship with God and leads you toward the most subtle pitfall awaiting the unwary Teacher: becoming nothing more than a speaker.

Some of the men I disciple are at the Teacher stage. Some serve as youth pastors; others are business professionals working nine to five. All of them lead a Bible study and disciple at least one other person. I tell them the same thing: don't fall for the trap of reading Scripture just to have something to share with the group. Falling into that routine will choke out your relationship with God. You'll become just a speaker.

Turn on the television or pick up a book by many of the popular preachers today, and you'll see what I mean. What they're saying sounds good and seems helpful. But on closer inspection, much of what is being offered is little more than self-help advice with a few Scripture verses wrapped around it. Good preaching is motivational, but a good motivational presentation is not necessarily good preaching. Take a look at what they're trying to motivate you to do. Materialism has become a huge problem in the church, not just for parishioners, but also for many of the clergy. Much of it centers on preachers who have become nothing but motivational speakers.

> No one can serve two masters. Either he will hate the one and
> love the other, or he will be devoted to the one and despise the
> other. You cannot serve both God and Money. (Matthew 6:24)

Scripture tells us that after Pentecost, the first-century church was quite the opposite.

Everyone was filled with awe, and many wonders and miraculous
signs were done by the apostles. All the believers were together
and had everything in common. Selling their possessions and
goods, they gave to anyone as he had need. (Acts 2:43–45)

Each one according to their need, not according to their wants. That's
a lot different from what we see today with megachurch pastors living in
huge mansions and flying around on private jets. But not everyone has
given himself over to materialism.

Most of you have heard of Rick Warren, pastor of Saddleback
Church in Southern California.[3] He began that church with a group that
met in a high school auditorium. Gradually the church grew to a weekly
attendance of more than ten thousand. Along the way Warren wrote *The
Purpose Driven Life,* which sold millions of copies.[4] As you would imagine, sales of that book generated a tremendous income stream. Rather
than spend it on himself or hoard it for the future, though, he took an in-
novative approach.

Rick and his wife always had tithed faithfully from their income, giving more than 10 percent to the church. But with the success of his books,
instead of giving away 10 percent and keeping 90 percent, they turned it
around. They now give away 90 percent and live on what's left. He also
stopped taking a salary. Rick is a Teacher who got it right. Those who
know him say he still drives the same old car, lives in the same house, and
takes visitors to the same local café, just as he did before he found material success.

Rick has become well known in recent years. Someone you might not
know as well is Walt Kallestad. Walt is pastor of Community Church of
Joy in Glendale, Arizona, a suburb of Phoenix.[5] When he arrived there in
1978, the church had about two hundred members. Under his leadership
the congregation grew to a weekly attendance of ten thousand. Then in

2002 Walt suffered a heart attack. He survived but only after major by-
pass surgery. Recuperating meant slowing down, and while he was confined to his home, the Holy Spirit began to confront Walt about the
nature of the church.

"You have been operating a religious retail store."

As Walt examined the church, he realized things had gotten off track.
They weren't making disciples. They were offering sound biblical sermons
and authentic worship on Sundays, but the success of the church was
built around attracting new attendees each week. When he was able to return to work full-time, he set about making changes. As a result many of
his staff members left. A large number of his congregation did too. It was
tough for a while, but the new direction changed the nature of the church
from merely offering a Sunday experience to discipling individuals. Walt
is a Teacher who got it right. It wasn't easy. It wasn't painless. It wasn't
without risk. Obedience requires the fortitude to change direction when
things get off mission. Walt found the courage to do that.

Matthew Barnett, at the Dream Center in Los Angeles, is another
Teacher who got it right.[6] He had a simple approach to ministry: just love
on people and encourage them to share Christ's love with others. If you
attend worship services there, you might find yourself sitting next to a
former alcoholic, drug addict, or prostitute, and by *former,* I mean just in
off the street the night before.

The Dream Center has a number of unique programs. My favorite
is their bus ministry. When you hear "bus ministry," it's easy to think of
a used school bus that travels through the neighborhood, picking up people and bringing them to church. The Dream Center does that in reverse.
They bring the church to the neighborhood. One bus ministry delivers
food. Another bus cruises the streets at night, picking up prostitutes, alcoholics, and street people. They bring them back to the church's facili-

ties and provide them with a shower, a meal, and a place to stay. In the process they model for them the love of Christ.

Dream Center's third bus ministry takes worship services on the road. The bus becomes a stage with a sound system and all the necessary equipment. Everyone who rides on the bus participates in leading the service. They park in the projects, transform the bus into a ministry center, and invite people to worship God.

As a result of the Dream Center's success, Matthew was offered a prime-time spot on a major religious television network. When he told me about it, I said, "Great."

He shook his head. "I turned them down."

"Turned them down?" I was surprised. "Why'd you do that? That sounds like a pretty big opportunity to impact people."

"It would have cost me my bus ministry," he replied, "because of the expense of being on television. We'd have to stop the bus ministry to do it. I can't stop the bus ministry." He shook his head. "That's not an option."

Rick, Walt, and Matthew avoided the trap of becoming mere speakers by maintaining a close, vibrant relationship with the Lord and by allowing Him to constantly examine their hearts. Jesus doesn't call Teachers to be motivational speakers; He calls them to make the Word known to a lost and dying world through a life of sacrificial service.

THE VICTORIES OF A TEACHER

The victory of Teachers comes when the process of spiritual maturity takes them so deeply into God and into themselves that the Holy Spirit is "in them and on them." They become sensitive enough to hear what God is telling them and obedient enough to give God's words to others.

They reach a point where ministry in the Spirit is no longer a struggle but a natural expression of the Holy Spirit's presence in their lives.

Victory for Teachers also comes when they are able to reach back two stages and pull someone up to the next stage. I said earlier that an Example is one who can bring a Wanderer or Wonderer up to the Believer stage. Teachers can sometimes reach Unbelievers, but not often. Wonderers and Wanderers don't want to hear words; they want to see action. Because of this, a Teacher is most effective in working with young Believers.

A good Teacher with a new Believer can bring that Believer up to the next stage in a powerful way. While I was in college, I worked with a number of students who already believed. We didn't have to talk about salvation. We went straight to a discussion about how Jesus walked, what He said, how He acted, and how He loved. It didn't take long for those Believers to become Examples.

CHAPTER 13

Peter as a Teacher

It was the best of times,
it was the worst of times.
—CHARLES DICKENS, *A TALE OF TWO CITIES*

The night Jesus was arrested was the worst night of Peter's life. Worse than the crucifixion that would happen shortly thereafter, and worse than anything Peter would experience in the years to come. That night, standing by the fire in the courtyard outside the temple, the disciple said things and did things he never thought he would say or do.

Peter had watched Jesus perform miracles and had seen miracles performed in Jesus' name by his own hand. He became an Example and a Teacher among the twelve disciples. Then he fell into the trap. He had progressed so far in maturity as a follower of Jesus that he started believing he no longer needed to pray. While Jesus found it necessary to pray that night in the Garden of Gethsemane, Peter went to sleep. When the moment of Jesus' greatest trial came, when Jesus was agonizing in prayer to His Father, Peter failed Him. Later in the night, when Peter was identified in the temple courtyard as a follower of Jesus, he denied Him. Peter had slept when he should have been praying, and he later denied his Master three times.

That sense of failure and confusion continued even after the resurrection. After seeing Jesus raised from the dead, you would think Peter and the other disciples would be telling everyone what had happened. Instead, they were fearful, disoriented, and unsure about what to do next. They languished in indecision until finally Peter took action. With the fate of Christendom hanging in the balance, he announced, "I'm going out to fish" (John 21:3). After all that had happened, he had to go back to where he began, working with a net on a boat in the Sea of Galilee.

But Jesus wasn't about to let the story end there. The gospel of John tells us that Peter, James, John, and four other disciples did, indeed, go fishing. And while they were on the water, Jesus appeared to them (see John 21:1, 4–14). He was standing on the shore, watching while the disciples who had been closest to Him worked the nets. They had already fished all night but had caught nothing.

So Jesus said to them, "Throw your net on the right side of the boat and you will find some" (John 21:6). They heard His words, and just as they had done many times before, they humbled themselves to Jesus and did as He said. What follows is a beautiful scene of redemption and restoration as Jesus restored Peter to the faith and, with him, the others as well.

These disciples, who had decided to return to fishing, threw the net on the opposite side of the boat, and it was filled with fish. As they pulled the bulging net ashore, Jesus waited for them with breakfast cooking over a fire.

And after the meal, Jesus looked at Peter and asked, "Peter, do you love me?"

Peter answered, "Yes, Lord."

And Jesus told him, "Feed my lambs" (verse 15, author's paraphrase).

Jesus asked Peter the same question two more times, and each time Peter gave the same response. "Yes, Lord, you know that I love you" (see verses 15–17).

With each question and with each of Peter's responses, Jesus was restoring Peter to faith. Everything that Peter had undone in the temple courtyard was being addressed and wiped away. This was raw in Peter's heart. He had stood outside the high priest's home, warming his hands over a fire, and denied Jesus three times. Now, after the resurrection, Peter stood on the shore next to a fire while Jesus wiped away his fear. As Jesus asked Peter to feed His lambs, He was bringing Peter up from a stumbling, imperfect Example to a powerful Teacher.

It is clear to everyone that Peter wasn't perfect. He was the only apostle that Jesus referred to as "Satan" (see Mark 8:33). But Jesus wasn't looking for a perfect follower; He wanted Peter's heart. And Jesus got Peter's heart in full that morning on the shore where their story together had begun more than three years earlier (see Matthew 4:18–20). Jesus had called the fisherman to follow Him; on this day He was reclaiming a fisherman who would follow Him to the death.

Later, after the Holy Spirit came upon the disciples at Pentecost (see Acts 1:4–5, 8; 2:1–4), Peter stood in the street and preached to a crowd about Jesus. Bold and forceful, he explained to his listeners what had happened in the Upper Room when the Holy Spirit fell upon them like tongues of fire. In describing that experience, Peter turned to the prophet Joel and said, "These men are not drunk, as you suppose. It's only nine in the morning! No, this is what was spoken by the prophet Joel" (Acts 2:15–16).

The Holy Spirit had come upon the followers of Jesus, just as Joel had prophesied. The Spirit of God was "in them and on them." Peter began preaching and boldly proclaimed the death, resurrection, and deity of Christ (see Acts 2:22–24, 36). He affirmed Jesus' teaching about Himself: "I and the Father are one" (John 10:30).

Thousands of people in the crowd welcomed the message, but the Jewish religious leadership considered such teaching to be heresy. Judaism was first and foremost a monotheistic faith. "Hear, O Israel: The LORD our God, the LORD is one" (Deuteronomy 6:4).

After encountering Jesus following the resurrection, Peter became the selfless Teacher Jesus had called him to be. And after receiving the Spirit of God at Pentecost, Peter was ready to impart the ways and works of Jesus to others. Peter would never again deny his Lord. He would instead be a bold and fearless Imparter. He would appear before the Sanhedrin to answer for his sermons and the claims he made about Jesus.

Peter was not a first-century version of a motivational speaker. He was a man on a mission, proclaiming the message of Jesus and risking his life to do it. He'd gone from his worst day to his best day, and the world would never be the same as a result.

PART 5

The Imparter

God did extraordinary miracles through Paul, so that even handkerchiefs and aprons that had touched him were taken to the sick, and their illnesses were cured and the evil spirits left them.

—ACTS 19:11–12

As a result, people brought the sick into the streets and laid them on beds and mats so that at least Peter's shadow might fall on some of them as he passed by. Crowds gathered also from the towns around Jerusalem, bringing their sick and those tormented by evil spirits, and all of them were healed.

—ACTS 5:15–16

CHAPTER 14

Called to Be an Imparter

Let me inherit a double portion of your spirit.

—ELISHA, SON OF SHAPHAT (2 KINGS 2:9)

Elijah was one of the greatest of the Hebrew prophets. He seemed to have power that, at least in some measure, was subject to his personal control. He said things and did things at his own initiative that required God's intervention. These amazing things came to pass just as Elijah said they would, yet he set them in motion without consulting God first. Elijah told King Ahab there would be no rain, and a drought ensued (see 1 Kings 17:1). A few years later God told Elijah to present himself to the king, and it started raining again (see 1 Kings 18:1).

He is the prophet of God who faced off against the prophets of Baal. He proved God's power and sovereignty by calling down fire from heaven to burn logs and a sacrifice that had been drenched in water. In fact, the fire of God consumed the stones of the altar, the logs on the altar, the soil, the sacrifice, *and* the water standing in a trench encircling the altar (see 1 Kings 18:22–39). Elijah called on God to reveal Himself in front of the people after the Baal prophets had spent the day trying to get their pagan god to send fire to burn their sacrifice.

This is the prophet who met with Jesus and Moses on the Mount of Transfiguration (see Luke 9:28–31). Elijah, at the end of his life, went to heaven without dying (see 2 Kings 2:11). When Jesus asked His disciples who people believed He was, it came to light that many Jews of the early first century thought Jesus was Elijah returned to earth (see Mark 8:28).

Elijah was a prophet without equal, performing unheard-of miracles and standing up for God in ways no other prophet had done before. And yet, in the course of his ministry, he discipled others. One of his favorite students was a man named Elisha, who first appears in 1 Kings (see 19:16). There, God told Elijah to anoint Elisha as his successor. For the remainder of his life, Elijah poured his teaching, his mentoring, and his life into Elisha, showing him all that he had seen and done and learned.

As Elijah neared the end of his life, Elisha stayed even closer by Elijah's side. Several times Elijah tried to separate himself from Elisha, but each time Elisha insisted on staying with him. Then as they were on their way to Gilead, Elijah turned to Elisha and said, "Tell me, what can I do for you before I am taken from you?"

Elisha replied, "Let me inherit a double portion of your spirit" (2 Kings 2:9).

As mysterious as Elijah's life was to this point, his response was even more so. He said, "You have asked a difficult thing. Yet if you see me when I am taken from you, it will be yours—otherwise not" (verse 10).

If a disciple asked us for a double portion of God's Spirit, most of us would say, "It's not mine to give. Let me pray for you." But not Elijah. He acknowledged that Elisha's request was troublesome, but then in the next sentence he agreed to the request (with one condition). Scripture doesn't say that God told Elijah to do that. It doesn't even say Elijah consulted with God on the matter. And it doesn't say God agreed to it.

THE POWER IN ELIJAH'S LIFE

The Bible is filled with accounts of a leader, prophet, or other believer asking God for direction or an answer in a particular situation and God's giving specific instructions. When God was bringing the plagues upon Egypt, Moses and Aaron were told what to say to Pharaoh, then they did as instructed (see Exodus 7–11). In the wilderness, after the Hebrews were set free from Egyptian captivity, the people needed water. Moses asked God about it, and God told him what to do. Moses did as God instructed, and water came from a rock (see Exodus 17:1–7).

Joshua was leading the army of Israel against Jericho. He was a great leader, but Joshua didn't come up with the plan of attack. God told him how to do it and what to say, and Joshua did just as he was instructed (see Joshua 5:13–6:27). The same thing happened at Ai. God told Joshua precisely how to attack, then Joshua commanded the army to carry out God's battle plan (see Joshua 8:1–29).

But none of those examples applies to Elijah's response to Elisha. When Elisha asked for a double portion of the Spirit that had come upon Elijah, the prophet agreed to the request on one condition. Fulfilling the request would require God's intervention, but Elijah failed to consult God in advance.

Not long after this exchange, as the prophets continued across the Jordan River to Gilead, chariots swooped down from heaven and took Elijah from the earth. As he rose into the clouds, he left behind his cloak. Elisha picked it up, wrapped himself in it, and started back toward the Jordan. When he reached the river, he took the cloak from his shoulders, rolled it up, and struck the river with it. As he swung the cloak toward the water, he said, "Where now is the LORD, the God of Elijah?" (2 Kings 2:14).

As soon as the cloak touched the water, the river parted, and Elisha crossed to the opposite side. He didn't hold a long prayer meeting. Instead, he spoke those simple words: "Where now is the LORD, the God of Elijah?"

ELISHA INHERITS A DOUBLE PORTION

Elisha went on to have a more powerful ministry than Elijah. Some of the things he did were rather troubling. Once, as he was going to Bethel, a group of children ran along with him, jeering, "Go on up, you baldhead!" When Elisha had heard enough, he turned to them and invoked a curse. Two bears came out of the woods and mauled them (see 2 Kings 2:23–25).

Another time, one of the young prophets who followed Elisha died. The man's widow faced financial ruin. Creditors were coming to take two of her sons in payment for the family's debts. Elisha didn't take up an offering for her. He simply asked,

"What do you have in your house?"

"Your servant has nothing there at all," she said, "except a little oil."

Elisha said, "Go around and ask all your neighbors for empty jars. Don't ask for just a few. Then go inside and shut the door behind you and your sons. Pour oil into all the jars, and as each is filled, put it to one side." (2 Kings 4:2–4)

The woman did as Elisha told her. Then she sold the oil and paid off her debts with the proceeds. The family lived off the money that was left.

In Shunem, Elisha met a wealthy woman who gave him a place to stay and meals to eat. Touched by her kindness, he asked what he could do for her. His servant, Gehazi, told him she had all she needed, except for a son. By then, the woman was too old to bear children. Elisha called her in and said, "About this time next year, you will hold a son in your arms." And it happened (see 2 Kings 4:8–17).

When you read the Bible's account of Elisha's life and ministry, you see what it looks like when a servant of God receives a double portion of God's Spirit. Here are a few more examples:

- One hundred men were fed with twenty loaves of bread, and after they ate, there was food left over (see 2 Kings 4:42–44).
- Naaman was cured of leprosy (see 2 Kings 5:1–14).
- A lost ax head, made of iron, floated in the river (see 2 Kings 6:4–7).

Just as Elijah moved forward with bold and miraculous acts, at times without first consulting with God, we see that Elisha likewise made use of power that seemed to be present with him and subject to his discretion.

THE HOLY SPIRIT IN YOUR LIFE

If you're like most people, you've always thought that power—the presence of the Holy Spirit "in you and on you"—is reserved for only a few of Jesus' followers. Perhaps you also believe that the Holy Spirit working through a person with such power was limited to believers in ancient times. If you think the Holy Spirit's work has such limitations, listen to what Peter said after Pentecost:

> Repent and be baptized, every one of you, in the name of Jesus Christ for the forgiveness of your sins. And you will receive the gift of the Holy Spirit. The promise is for you and your children and for all who are far off—for all whom the Lord our God will call. (Acts 2:38–39)

In the days that followed, Peter healed a beggar who couldn't walk. The man lay near the temple gates, and Peter chose to heal him. He didn't first call a long prayer service; he simply uttered these words: "Silver or gold I do not have, but what I have I give you. In the name of Jesus Christ of Nazareth, walk." The man jumped to his feet and entered the temple "walking and jumping, and praising God" (Acts 3:6, 8).

The miraculous power at Peter's disposal also appeared for purposes of judgment. Ananias and Sapphira, husband and wife, sold a piece of property and brought the proceeds to the apostles. Ananias gave the impression that the monetary gift represented the entire amount they had received from the sale of their property. In fact, what he brought was only a portion of what they had received.

Peter didn't give him a long lecture. He simply told Ananias—who had arrived ahead of his wife—that he knew about the lie. Then he said, "You have not lied to men but to God." At those words Ananias dropped dead.

When Sapphira arrived later, Peter asked her about the offering. She told the same story as Ananias. Peter's reply was simple. "The feet of the men who buried your husband are at the door, and they will carry you out also" (Acts 5:4, 9). She dropped dead immediately.

Displays of miraculous power did not stop there but continued in Peter's life and in the lives of many others. Philip was physically transported in the Spirit, leaving one place and suddenly appearing in another (see Acts 8:39). Paul, struck blind on the road to Damascus, had his sight restored by another man named Ananias, merely by the sound of the man's voice and the touch of his hands (see Acts 9:1–19).

Not everyone we read about in the New Testament saw that kind of power made evident in their lives. And today, not every Christian will be favored by God with such power. But some are favored in this way. The person with this kind of power is what I call an Imparter.

IMPARTING GOD'S PRESENCE AND BLESSING

Like Elijah, Elisha, Peter, and others, an Imparter has the ability not only to enjoy the presence of God "in him and on him" but to impart that presence and blessing to others. That really isn't ability but favor—the favor of God.

I don't believe that God favors some of His followers and doesn't favor others. He favors *all* His children. But not all are favored in the same way. Some receive God's direct favor, and others are blessed by the spillover. Remember the story we looked at earlier when Peter and six other disciples decided to go back to fishing. They worked all night on the Sea of Galilee without catching anything. Then Jesus said, "Throw your net on the right side of the boat and you will find some" (John 21:6). When they did that, they found the net was so full of fish they had trouble hauling it in.

Jesus had sought out Peter. He waited on the shore for the men to bring their boat in. Peter, who had denied Christ and was racked by fears, needed to be confronted with Jesus' power over *all* things—sickness, demons, death, and the laws of nature. Jesus is Lord over all, and at that moment Peter needed a demonstration of Christ's power that would remind him of that truth.

The miracle that Jesus performed that morning was meant for Peter to see. But the favor that Jesus showed Peter spilled over to the others. This is an example of the anointing of God that is on one follower of Jesus and spilling over to his or her neighbors.

The encounter with Jesus restored Peter's faith and established him to enter into his calling in God's Kingdom. Jesus favored Peter with a miracle and a blessing—a net filled with fish after a night of futility. And in favoring Peter, Jesus blessed the disciples who were fishing with him. They all received a spillover blessing because of their relationship with Peter.

This is how the life of an Imparter works. God pours His anointing on the Imparter. That anointing comes with such power that those who are close to the Imparter become drenched in the overflow. God does not favor only a few of us, but He does favor some differently than others.

Jesus was an Imparter while He lived on earth. The effect of His presence, words, teachings, and favor is illustrated in his conversation with the two believers who walked along the road to Emmaus. They encountered a Man they didn't recognize. As the Stranger walked with them, He noticed how sad they were. He asked what had happened, and they told about the death of Jesus, their Master. They shared the sorrow of their dashed hopes. When they reached the village, the believers invited the Stranger to eat with them. While they ate supper, Scripture says, "their eyes were opened and they recognized him, and he disappeared from their sight" (Luke 24:31). After Jesus left them, they said, "Were not our hearts burning within us while he talked with us on the road and opened the Scriptures to us?" (verse 32).

Their hearts were burning from the words of Jesus. Those whom Jesus favors to be Imparters have a similar effect on others. Their life and the presence of the Holy Spirit "in them and on them" make the Imparters' presence a miraculous moment. Imparters allow others to see God at a new and higher level and make them want more of God.

MIRACLES IN UNREACHED REGIONS

Heidi Baker is a Christian and an Imparter. She and her husband, Rolland, launched Iris Ministries in 1980 and began ministering in Mozambique in 1995. Iris has grown to include more than five thousand churches in Mozambique and neighboring countries. Nearly two thousand orphans are cared for in Iris centers.

Heidi and Rolland conduct outreaches in Africa and beyond, and they have a special burden to minister in unreached areas. God's favor is on them, and when Heidi speaks and teaches from the Bible, God does supernatural work through her.

A woman attended one of Heidi's conferences on a night when she was teaching on love. About a month earlier the same woman had become a Christian in a meeting where Heidi was speaking. On this night, however, the woman showed up to get away from her home. She was married to an abusive alcoholic, and he had died earlier that day. The woman was glad that her husband was dead, and instead of burying him right away, she left his body lying in the bed where he had died. She then left to go to the conference.

That night the woman was convicted by the Holy Spirit and the Word of God as Heidi taught about love. After listening to Heidi's teaching, the woman told her friends she needed to be obedient to God—to love people and pray for them. She realized she needed to love her husband even though he had been abusive. She went home from the meeting and laid hands on his body, and her husband rose up. The next day she took her husband with her to the conference, and he gave his life to Jesus.

This is the favor of God that spills over from an Imparter to other people. The overflow of God's favor on Heidi's life blessed the woman who came to hear her teach and then extended to the woman's dead husband.

At another conference in Africa, a woman from a tribe of cannibals attended one of the meetings. Earlier in the day, before she arrived at the meeting site, the woman had a terrible argument with her family. When she set out from home, she was so angry that she decided when she returned that night, she would dine on a family member's flesh.

At the conference, after having decided to exact violence against an offending family member, she listened to Heidi teach from the Scriptures.

At the end of the meeting, Heidi came down into the audience and walked straight to the woman. Heidi hugged the woman and told her that God loved her.

The woman reported that she had never felt love like that before. She decided to go back home and forgive her family. One hug in the presence of God touched an angry, unforgiving, violent woman. The love of God imparted by Heidi Baker changed this woman's life completely.

When the imparting gift is on you, something that might seem ordinary (a hug, a prayer, a spoken word) is taken by the Lord and used to do His supernatural work. The unexplainable happens. That is the life of an Imparter.[1]

CHAPTER 15

Trials, Traps, and Victories

When Peter came to Antioch, I opposed him to his face, because he was clearly in the wrong.

—PAUL, THE APOSTLE (GALATIANS 2:11)

A ll my life I have read about people in the Bible who saw miracles take place at the sound of their voice. They spoke, and God showed up. Growing up, I'd hear people in church talk about miracles, but I never saw anyone stand up and say to a sick person, "Be healed."

There is a difference between talking about the possibility of miracles taking place or saying you believe that miracles still happen and being an Imparter—a person God uses to do His supernatural work. An Imparter is one whose words or actions can ignite God's healing and life-changing power in a situation. That person has stepped into the anointing of Elijah, the double portion of Elisha, and the spiritual power of the apostles at Pentecost.

Imparting the ways and works of Jesus is exciting. But it brings its own trials, traps, and victories. You need to know that when you minister from the fullness of the Holy Spirit, you can expect intense opposition.

Enduring the trials, overcoming the traps, and reaching the victory of the Imparter take you to unimaginable maturity in Christ.

THE TRIALS OF AN IMPARTER

The trials of an Imparter come in three flavors. For males, it's Gold, Glory, and Girls. And for females, it's Gold, Glory, and Gents. One of my mentors called these trials the Three Gs, because they are Satan's generals.

Gold represents the attraction of money and possessions. It will cause you to chase fleeting, material pleasure and riches at the cost of your soul and your credibility. If you give in to the lure of possessions and money, you will give up your position as a soldier for the Kingdom of God. You can't serve mammon and still be a servant of Christ.

Money is more powerful than we like to admit, and its voice is seductive. "Your gifts are amazing," it will tell you. "You should get paid serious money for coming and sharing those gifts." Gold says to you, "If they can't give you this much money to come and minister, you shouldn't go." It all sounds perfectly reasonable on the one hand, since "the worker deserves his wages" (1 Timothy 5:18). On the other hand, it sounds like a hard-nosed contract negotiation. Once your focus shifts to the things you *want*, your eyes are no longer on the priority of your calling. You aren't ministering out of your calling; you're negotiating terms of your employment. You then stop being a servant of Christ and become a mere hireling.

When Elvis Presley began singing, he traveled the southeastern United States with two other musicians. They played almost every night, sometimes in nice venues and sometimes in dives. They traveled by car, often sleeping in it or on a friend's sofa. They didn't mind eating beans out of a can and drinking from a water hose at a service station. The hardships were worth it, because they were following their dream.

But later, after they achieved success on stage, on the radio, on television, and on the record charts, they had more money than they could imagine. Elvis and his entourage got caught up in the things money could buy. A single-minded devotion to that privileged lifestyle plagued him the remainder of his life.

I'm not saying that Elvis started out as a servant of Jesus. I'm simply using his life as an example of the lure of money and possessions. He started out using his incredible talent because of a passion for music and a desire to entertain people. His shift from singing for the love of it to chasing more and more money and fame demonstrates how a person can start with the right kind of ambition only to be entrapped by the lowest desires.

As a Christian who is maturing in Christ, just because you attain a certain level of spiritual maturity doesn't mean you can stop there and start coasting. And it doesn't mean you are no longer vulnerable to the lowest desires that present themselves.

Jesus said, "Foxes have holes and birds of the air have nests, but the Son of Man has no place to lay his head" (Matthew 8:20). The calling of God on your life isn't about money or possessions. In fact, your calling will at times move you to uncomfortable places with your money, where your only place of comfort is in God.

The lure of glory

The second trial that comes to Imparters is that of glory. There's an old adage that says, "There's no limit to what you can do if you don't mind who gets the credit." In the life and ministry of an Imparter, the One getting the credit is God, not you. Finding yourself being lured by glory is in line with the unrighteous ambition of Satan before humans were created.

Satan, also known as Lucifer, was the most beautiful angel of all and one of the most powerful. He commanded a large company of angels, but that wasn't enough to satisfy him. When he heard that humanity was being created—and being created in the image of God—he couldn't stand it. He felt that he should have the glory. But instead, a new human creature was being introduced. And these humans would possess the very image of God, stamped on their soul and spirit.

Lucifer decided he couldn't let that happen. (Of course, he couldn't prevent it, but he gave it a try.) Spurred on by his ego, he made a play to throw down God and take control of heaven. In the end he was the one who got thrown down.

Pride is a destructive force. It runs counter to the selflessness that is learned in the Example stage. Pride is the exact opposite of the servant-shepherd model of ministry taught and lived out by Jesus. Regardless of your level of maturity, you are called to live as Jesus lived. You might never achieve that goal, but it is your goal nevertheless. Bringing your lifestyle into conformity with His is a process of eliminating everything that runs counter to His character qualities. Pride is one of the first things that has to go.

Not long ago I spoke at a men's conference. When I was finished, I asked the group if anyone had something they wanted to talk about. A guy stood up and said, "Shaun, do you prepare to speak the way you prepare for a game?"

I said, "I get pretty excited for both."

The man shook his head. "No, I mean like the night before. What did you do the night before you spoke to us?"

I laughed and looked around the room. "Is everyone in here married?" They all leaned in for the answer. "Last night my wife had some friends over. After they left, she walked over to me and said, 'Babe, I know you have that men's conference tomorrow, but do you mind staying up and doing the dishes?' So, to answer your question, last night I was doing the dishes."

To have the character of God, you must take your name out of the equation and off the marquee. Pride has to be the first thing to go.

The lure of the opposite sex

The other major trial that an Imparter faces is the third G, what I have called Girls or Gents. This general of Satan stirs the lust of the flesh, which goes beyond the temptation to have sex with someone who isn't your husband or wife. This general attacks anything that can please your flesh and get you off of following Christ. We live in a sexually obsessed culture, and this trial only gets worse the further you grow toward spiritual maturity. Men and women in positions of power and authority face this every day. The Imparter in the Kingdom of God is never immune from this trial.

Power is an aphrodisiac. When you occupy a position of authority or have a high profile in what you do, you suddenly become more interesting and appealing to members of the opposite sex. Women can find the most unattractive men irresistible. When an ordinary-looking man is elevated to an office or position of power, he finds that things change dramatically. Although in the past he never got a second look from women, suddenly he finds that he has become irresistible. The same phenomenon is common in the experience of women who are average looking and who achieve prominent and influential roles or offices. Previously they did not attract men, but now they find they're pursued like starlets.

When you achieve a level of prominence, wealth, or power, it also blinds the eyes of others to your flaws. A person with great ability can have a detestable personality and corrupt ethics. He or she can have a deeply flawed character and a near total lack of morals and still be admired and honored. No matter that the person is a jerk and is using his or her status for personal advancement; people will still follow that person and heap praise on him or her. It's easy for a leader to accept the blind praise of eager followers and be oblivious to his or her own pride.

This is the trial of the Imparter. The person is lifted up so high and is so admired that it's easy to listen to the third attacking general of Satan. Satan's attacker will say to the Imparter, "Now you can feel free to be a jerk to people. And go ahead and flirt with any man or woman who catches your eye. Enjoy yourself and indulge your pleasures. After all, you're somebody!"

Pride and pleasure can destroy you

The sports world is filled with stories about off-the-field exploits of its stars. During my years in the NFL, I heard about players who succumbed to the temptation of women who would approach them at the team hotel or at the stadium. I'd watch a fellow player go off with a strange woman on his arm, knowing where they were going and what they were about to do. I knew that going through with such a thing would cost that man everything: his name, reputation, peace of mind, wife, children, and home.

Moving up in spiritual maturity toward the likeness of Christ is the goal of every Christian, but along with that growth comes increasing trials and temptations. The anointing and favor of God rest on the Imparter. Satan is aware of that, and he will not stop until he has made his evil counteroffer to try to get the Imparter to trade God's favor for a moment's pleasure.

It comes down to a matter of commitment, priorities, and focus. The gifts and favor an Imparter receives come from God and naturally seek to glorify the Lord, not the Imparter. By contrast, Satan offers the opportunity to rise to a position that puts the spotlight on the person and not on God. It's a lie that promises to make you the star in place of God. It is an elevated position from which it is very difficult to wash the feet of others and to be the servant of all.

The Holy Spirit's presence attracts people to Christ. In the process many will be attracted to the Imparter. Satan will tempt you in order to produce confusion. He will lie to you by saying that, as you serve God, you deserve some pleasure along the way. He will offer abundant opportunities to fulfill the desires of your flesh. The three trials—Gold, Glory, and Girls (or Gents)—are sent from Satan to destroy you.

So stand up. Trials and temptations will come, but remember Jesus was tempted in every way, yet He did not fall (see Hebrews 4:15).

THE TRAPS OF AN IMPARTER

Imparters are not given a special ability to avoid traps, and the biggest one is fear. Everyone deals with fear at some level, but fear is the one thing that can stop an Imparter from moving into the fullness of ministry in Christ. When the Holy Spirit speaks, Imparters have a choice. They can act on what they hear, or they can refuse. Imparters are sent to impart; that is their purpose and calling. They bring the tangible, powerful presence of God to individuals, groups, and circumstances. But when they allow fear to inhibit their obedience, they cut off God's ability to work through them.

Fear often comes in a subtle way. You notice someone and you think, *I should say something to that person.* You know exactly what you should say. Or you see someone, and you know you should step out boldly and pronounce healing over that person. Or you know you should give that person a word of admonishment or a word of encouragement. Then Satan starts to play with you. You struggle with fear, and if you give in to it, you will be preventing the fullness of the Holy Spirit from ministering through you. Fear can stop the work of Imparters who have heard from God but choose not to act.

The first question you often hear is this one: "Is this really God I'm hearing, or is it just me?" Then your mind starts to work on you. "I don't want to embarrass anyone. I don't want to embarrass myself."

Or you start rationalizing your fear. "God is a God of order, and He is not forceful. He won't push me into an awkward situation." This one sounds really good. It takes the truth (God is a God of order) and pairs it with an erroneous implication (God would not embarrass me). God is a God of order, but He doesn't really care whether you're completely comfortable or not. He's going to do through you whatever He determines to do at whatever time He determines to do it. Your part is to obey and be a channel for His favor, His blessing, and His work in the other person's life.

It is important to discern the voice that is speaking—God's or your own. You must distinguish between the two so you know which voice to feed. The difference is in the direction each of the two voices wants to take you. Your own voice, which is influenced by the flesh, will take you toward your self. But the voice of the Holy Spirit directs you toward others.

The trap of silent struggles and sin

Imparters also face the trap of feeling like they can't confess their sins or struggles to anyone. The ministry of an Imparter is powerful and dynamic. Those who live at other levels of spiritual maturity sometimes confuse an Imparter's anointing with a flawless walk with God. The onlooker assumes that an Imparter who can do such amazing things for the Kingdom must be a person who never struggles or stumbles. That attitude is conveyed to the Imparter in not-so-subtle ways, and sometimes the Imparter begins to believe it's true. Imparters can reach a point where they feel they can no longer struggle since they have been called by God to impart His life to others. When that happens and when they do struggle with temptation and sin, they fall into the lie of thinking they can't admit their struggles. They believe they can't own up to stumbling and failing.

It is common for Imparters to fall for this trap. They rationalize that if they confess their sins or struggles, it will set a bad example or cause others to fall or perhaps cause people to think less of them. This is a deadly trap because it prevents confession—which is exactly what the enemy wants. Confession is necessary because it lets the light shine into the dark places and keeps Satan at bay. Without confession, Satan has access to us, and when he comes, he brings friends.

Paul told the Christians living in Corinth, "When I am weak, then I am strong" (2 Corinthians 12:10). To some, confessing struggles and sin might appear to be a sign of weakness. It might not meet their expectations of how an Imparter should act. But as we have seen, no one is above the need to honestly present themselves before God and others. Confession and honesty turn the light of truth on us and our circumstances and deprive Satan of power and influence. Satan thrives in darkness. If we live transparently in the light of God's truth and in our relationships with one another, God can be strong through us.

THE VICTORIES OF AN IMPARTER

The victory of Imparters comes when they are able to abide in the presence of God. The Imparter begins as a Teacher who experiences the anointing of God in certain situations as he or she is ministering to others. But as Imparters grow in maturity, they take all the gifts, powers, and anointing with them in all their work for the Kingdom. For instance, they might be in the grocery store and sense the Holy Spirit giving them a word for a fellow shopper. If the Imparter is obedient to God and speaks that word, it might shift the other person's life forever. Or a mother who is an Imparter might come home from work and find her daughter sick in bed. The mother prays for her daughter, and the girl gets up with no fever and no illness. That is victory, and it comes from living in the continual presence of God. The Holy Spirit anoints you, and the benefits of that anointing spill over to those around you.

Earlier we talked about those in the latter stages of spiritual maturity being able to minister in a powerful way to those who are two levels behind them. In keeping with that pattern, the Imparter's greatest effectiveness is in working with Christians who are Examples. The signs and wonders that are evident in the Imparter's ministry act as a witness and inspiration to the Example. The ministry of the Imparter says to the Example, "God really is alive and moving. His presence is real, powerful, and tangible." This ministry is important, because the Example and the Unbeliever (both the Wanderer and Wonderer) share something in common. They need to see God being present and active in real life rather than merely hear about it. God uses the Imparter to do that for the Example, demonstrating the power that is available to those who obey and mature in Christ.

At the same time, the presence of the Holy Spirit that the Imparter brings gives the Example an anointing that enables him or her to become a Teacher. That experience becomes the initial foundation of the new Teacher's message.

Imparters find that God uses them to minister to a wide range of people. Imparters do not just hope God will show up; they *know* God will show up through their anointing and calling. This book began with a dream I had of gathering with my teammates around an injured player, laying hands on him, and seeing him miraculously healed. People who are in tune with God look for opportunities to let God's favor spill over to minister to others. Because they look for God to work, they find that God is present in ways that are evident to all. God shows up in their ministry and performs miracles, signs, and wonders.

The mark of success for Christians is whether they are obedient to God's call upon their lives. Attention, praise, and a high profile are not the goals. But Imparters find that they reach far greater numbers for Christ, compared to the ministries of a new Believer, an Example, or a Teacher. Although they all have an audience and an obligation to make disciples, the dynamics involved in that process are quite different for the Imparter.

If you follow the game of football, you know that not all players on a team have the same level of talent. Some players are game changers. Their athletic ability produces a dramatic result. The game changer on offense is so good at what he does that the opposing defense has to adjust their formation and style of play to meet the challenge. Imparters are like that. They are game changers. They see and hear things from God that others do not, and their ability to minister through what they see permits the Holy Spirit to flow freely through them as He wills.

Those are the victories of the Imparter.

CHAPTER 16

Peter as an Imparter

> While Peter was still speaking these
> words, the Holy Spirit came on all who
> heard the message.
>
> —ACTS 10:44

P eter walked with another disciple, John, toward the temple in Jerusalem. As they made their way through the streets, he remembered the night Jesus had led them down those same streets to a hillside by the olive presses. He recalled the moment the authorities came to arrest Jesus and the things that happened in the courtyard outside the high priest's house. Guilt stabbed at his soul as he thought of what he'd said that night, denying his Master. Then, just as quickly, the guilt evaporated.

On the morning when Jesus appeared to the disciples on the shore of Galilee, the things Jesus said changed everything. Then, after Jesus ascended, His followers had gathered in an upper room to celebrate the Feast of Pentecost. In the same room where they had celebrated their final meal with Jesus, the Holy Spirit actually came on them. It seemed as though Jesus was in them and on them at the same time. They all remembered that Jesus had told them about this in advance.

I will ask the Father, and he will give you another Counselor to be with you forever—the Spirit of truth. The world cannot accept him, because it neither sees him nor knows him. But you know him, for he lives with you and will be in you. (John 14:16–17)

After God's Spirit came upon them, Peter referred to a last-days prophecy of Joel:

In the last days, God says,
  I will pour out my Spirit on all people.
Your sons and daughters will prophesy,
  your young men will see visions,
  your old men will dream dreams.
Even on my servants, both men and women,
  I will pour out my Spirit in those days,
  and they will prophesy.
I will show wonders in the heaven above
  and signs on the earth below.
    (Acts 2:17–19)

Now the Feast of Pentecost had passed, and Peter hurried to keep up with John. The city of Jerusalem was still alive with tourists and parties and merchants hawking their wares, but John seemed not to notice. He set a quick pace.

Peter and John had known each other most of their lives, first as children and then as fishermen in Capernaum. Now they were partners in leading a loosely organized band of Jews who had known Jesus, a group many were calling the Way. They had shared leading roles among the disciples while Jesus was alive, but now they were the ones to whom people turned for answers.

Peter glanced over at John. Since the morning three years earlier when

Jesus first noticed the fishermen and called them to follow Him, Peter had changed. And especially since the Pentecost experience, when the Holy Spirit came upon them, he had become a different man. He wasn't so pushy or so quick to speak without thinking. Peter chuckled to himself, thinking, *I was so boisterous.*

John interrupted Peter's thoughts. "You say something?"

"No." Peter glanced up. "Just thinking about Jesus."

"We came this way that last night, the night of His arrest."

"Yeah."

"It's okay, you know." John looked over at him. "No one thinks less of you."

"I think less of me."

"You shouldn't. We were all scared. Look at what happened. When the guards showed up, James almost knocked me down getting out of the way. I looked back, and there you were, standing your ground with your sword drawn."

Peter grinned. "You saw me take that guy's ear off?"

"I saw you swing for his head. He'd be dead if he hadn't ducked."

Suddenly John stopped and took Peter by the front of his robe. "Listen, you were brave. You were there. You went with Him. That was more than the rest of us did. So don't keep beating yourself up about it. Jesus forgave you. That's why He said those things to you that morning by the sea after He came back from the dead. Forgive yourself, and let's get on with it."

Tears filled Peter's eyes. He swallowed. John let go of him and slapped him on the shoulder. "Come on. We have things to do."

As was their custom when in Jerusalem, Peter was on his way to the temple for three o'clock prayers. He believed Jesus was the Messiah, but he also was a devout Jew. In his mind, observing the liturgy of daily prayers was not optional. And on that day John had asked to come with him.

As they walked through the gate outside the temple courtyard, they were met by two men carrying a third man between them. The man they carried had a leg that was shriveled. With a glance Peter knew the man had never been able to walk. Carefully the two men set the lame man near the temple gate and positioned him so that all who sought to enter the temple had to walk past him. As they propped him in place, the lame man glanced up at Peter and thrust out his hand.

"Something for the poor?"

Just then, Peter's heart burned. In his mind he heard the voice of Jesus: *Give him the bread that will change him forever.* He'd heard those words many times before, only this time the voice sounded like Peter's own. And it sounded like Jesus' at the same time. Deep inside, Peter came to the thudding realization that he could not simply pass by this man. He knew what he had to say.

As he approached the man, Peter heard another voice, reminding him of all that he had done wrong. *I know that you meant exactly what you said that night. You don't really know Jesus. You aren't that close to the Messiah. You just went along for the fun of it.*

As Peter struggled to push those thoughts aside, the lame man spoke again. "Something for the poor?"

Peter stopped and turned back to face him. "Look up here at me," he said. The man glanced up, then his eyes darted to the side as John stepped near. Peter leaned down and tapped the man on the shoulder. "Look at us."

The lame man looked up, anticipating a gift of money. His eyes sparkled at the possibility of getting something from both of the men. Instead, Peter smiled. "I don't have any gold. And I don't have any silver." The man's countenance fell. Peter continued. "But I have one thing you can never buy, and I'm going to give it to you for free."

Peter paused to take a breath. "In the name of Jesus Christ of Nazareth, get up and walk."

The man gave him a blank stare. Peter reached down and took him by the hand. "Get up." Peter tugged gently on the man's hand. "Stand up and walk."

The man brought one leg back and tucked it underneath his thigh, then pushed up. His ankles and feet had been weak since birth, but suddenly they were alive and strong. He grinned at Peter and looked over at John. "I can move my feet!" He stuck one leg out in front of him and turned his foot from side to side.

"I can move my feet!" he shouted. "I can move my feet!"

The man took a hop to the left, clapped his hands over his head, and spun around. "I can move my feet!" Jumping and shouting, he hurried up the stairs ahead of the apostles, calling at the top of his voice, "In the name of Jesus Christ of Nazareth! In the name of Jesus! I can move my feet!" (To read the biblical account of this event, see Acts 3:1–10.)

That was Peter the Imparter. As an apostle he was an impact player, a game changer. Following Pentecost and the outpouring of the Holy Spirit, the mere appearance of his shadow as it fell across the sick was enough to bring healing (see Acts 5:15).

Peter had his share of difficulties, and he would continue to face major challenges. But he always fought his way through and held on to the hope that Jesus had instilled in him. Peter saw many miracles performed through his ministry, a ministry that reached hundreds of thousands from Jerusalem all the way to Rome. Peter might have fallen harder than any of the other disciples the night when Jesus was arrested, but he came back even stronger. Following Pentecost, Peter became an Imparter—and through him, God changed the world.

PART 6

Walking the Walk

So he will fall down and worship God,
exclaiming, "God is really among you!"

—PAUL, THE APOSTLE (1 CORINTHIANS 14:25)

The powerful play goes on and you may
contribute a verse. What will your verse be?

—ROBIN WILLIAMS IN *DEAD POETS SOCIETY*

CHAPTER 17

In Order—
Out of Order

If you follow the recipe, the cake will
come out great.

—MOM (CAROL ALEXANDER)

Both on the football field and off, the power of order has amazed me. Nothing unleashes potential like putting the right person in the right place at the right time. There is no limit to what can be accomplished when everyone knows their job and follows instructions.

It is said that a great defense wins football games. Three of the greatest defenses in NFL history were the 1985 Chicago Bears, the 1960s and 1970s Minnesota Vikings Purple People Eaters, and the 2000 Baltimore Ravens. Many of the players on those teams ranked among the best who ever played the game, but the most amazing thing was the way they played beyond what was expected of them. They were always at the right place at the right time and doing the right thing.

When I played in the NFL, my goal each time I touched the ball was to change the pace of the game. To accomplish that, I did my best to force someone on the opposing team's defense to play out of position, leaving a gap I could run through. The week before a game, I studied films of our opponent's previous games and noted the timing of everything they did.

Then, as we ran plays at them during the game, I watched to see what happened. If I ran a play quickly, I noted their reaction and compared it to the reaction I got if I ran it slowly. I also studied each player across the line of scrimmage. After a while I knew which guy would take the bait and react to me by moving out of position, creating a hole in the defense. Paying attention to those details led to some of my biggest games.

Satan works on us in much the same way. He looks for holes to attack through. If none are obvious, he makes us move out of position to reveal gaps in our defenses. Sometimes he attacks us fast and from many different angles, hoping something will get through: a foothold, a loss of credibility, or, even worse, death.

On the football field, the team that stays focused and keeps all eleven guys doing their job on every play has no gaps. They make opposing teams fight for every yard and every first down. That is the power of order. Like a great defense, order puts you in position to stop corrupting spiritual attacks that would otherwise cause you to stumble.

Order can also create opportunities. In sports, the team that is bigger, faster, and more talented usually wins a lot of games, but not every game. With teamwork, a team that is weaker, smaller, and less talented can force the better team to play out of position. By minimizing the better team's strengths and forcing them to play in a way they're not accustomed to, the weaker team can win. That approach to teamwork is an example of the power of order.

Power comes through order in spiritual matters, helping you grow through the five stages and making you more fruitful in ministry. It also can work in the opposite direction, and the construction of the Tower of Babel is a vivid example. At that time in human history, everyone spoke the same language. With the advantage of a common language, the people came together to build a tower designed to reach all the way to heaven. Of course, they couldn't actually reach heaven, but their attempt to do so showed them the power of order. If they could organize themselves for that one glorious job, there was nothing they couldn't do (see Genesis 11:6). To stop them, God confused their language so they could no longer understand each other. He frustrated their attempts to establish the glory of humanity—as opposed to honoring God—by introducing *disorder*.

LIVING IN GOD'S ORDER

In the previous chapters we discussed God's order in the steps of growth to spiritual maturity. Those steps follow an established progression, beginning with the Unbeliever and continuing to Believer, Example, Teacher, and finally Imparter. Follow the order and you will grow to the full measure of spiritual maturity in each stage. But if you try to hurry the process by rushing through the stages or even skipping a stage, you will reap disorder. Like the frustrated efforts of the people who tried to build the Tower of Babel, confusion and error will plague your life and ministry.

Anyone can lead others to grow in maturity, no matter what level they are on or what level the other person is on. Sometimes God opens opportunities, and all He needs is a yes from you. After Paul was converted on the road to Damascus, he was struck blind. God sent a man named Ananias to pray for Paul to receive his sight. Ananias prayed, and Paul received his sight (see Acts 9:17–19).

That is the only mention of Ananias of Damascus in all of Scripture. He might have been a disciple who had grown to be an Imparter, and God simply pointed him in Paul's direction. But it's also possible that Ananias was a Believer trying to grow into an Example. He could have been either a Believer or an Example who was willing to say yes to God's direction when no one else would. After all, Paul had been persecuting Christians, and many Believers would have been reluctant to go near him. Ananias, however, said yes. And even if he never functioned again as an

Imparter, he did so on that day. You might find yourself in a similar position: called upon to minister in a capacity higher than your current walk.

God will use a Believer, an Example, or a Teacher who is willing to be used in order to get someone saved or to help someone walk closer to Him. And since God is sovereign, if He chooses to do so, He can use animals, inanimate objects, and even Unbelievers to do His work (see Mark 9:38–41). Most people are familiar with the story of Jonah, the man who refused to go to Nineveh as God's prophet. God used a great fish to swallow Jonah and keep him from running away from his duty (see Jonah 1:17). Many other examples are not as familiar but just as compelling:

- In the book of Hosea, God uses a sexually promiscuous wife and her betrayed husband as a powerful story of His love for His unfaithful children.
- Rahab was a prostitute living in enemy territory. She hid the Israelite spies who were scouting out Jericho prior to a war (see Joshua 2:1).
- Jesus told the Pharisees that if His disciples were to stop praising Him, then stones lying on the ground would cry out His praise (see Luke 19:39–40).
- In the Old Testament, God needed to get through to Balaam, so He used the man's donkey to speak a message (see Numbers 22:22–31).
- Even Pontius Pilate, a Roman official and certainly no follower of Jesus, ordered that the sign posted on Jesus' cross proclaim the truth: "Jesus of Nazareth, the King of the Jews" (John 19:19). When the Pharisees protested the wording, suggesting that Pilate qualify the assertion about Jesus' kingship, he replied, "What I have written, I have written" (verse 22).

These and other examples are the exceptions, to be sure. But it's clear that God will use the person who is in the right place and available for His

work. Knowing this should inspire us to keep pursuing a deeper relationship with God and not chase a structured format or official formula.
When God appears to step outside the order of the five stages of spiritual maturity and uses an unexpected servant to minister in an unusual
way, it should lead us to love God and continue to chase Jesus. Our goal
is to obey and serve God, not to pursue a formal structure of spiritual
growth.

However, for the most part, God will lead us and use us according to
the five stages of growth into Christlikeness.

MINISTERING WITH THE GREATEST EFFECTIVENESS

God has shown that the most powerful and most effective way to touch
lives is through practicing the order He established. And followers of Jesus
have the greatest effectiveness when they touch lives and help others grow
who are two stages behind. Consider the effect on the life of an Unbeliever
(both Wanderers and Wonderers) that a person in each of the stages of
growth can have.

Believers are almost always excited about finding salvation and coming to know Jesus. A Believer's fresh excitement will sometimes excite the
Wanderer and the Wonderer, but most of the time, their response to a Believer's excitement fizzles out. In that way, the Wanderer and the Wonderer are like the seed that fell on stony ground in Jesus' parable of the
sower. The seed springs up quickly but then just as quickly dies away (see
Matthew 13:1–23).

On the other hand, an Example has matured and mellowed some in
the faith. Examples express less outward, emotional excitement. Instead,
they have developed more consistent love for God and greater devotion
to God and to serving others. That lends authenticity to their walk, and

authenticity always leaves a mark on the Wanderer and the Wonderer. Unbelievers tend to watch Examples more closely than Believers. When a time of need arises or spiritual questions come to the surface, Unbelievers will seek out an Example to talk to. Wanderers and Wonderers want to understand how the Example lives, and why.

The Teacher, which is three stages beyond the Unbeliever, can be a source of great wisdom to the Unbeliever, especially the Wonderer. But if the Wonderer doesn't submit to the Teacher's leadership, or if he only gets Christian teaching at infrequent times, he eventually will come under attack.

Satan will tell the Wonderer, "Look around you. Everyone has sin in their life. They all have something they can't control and don't want to give up. So you can feel free to hold on to your own sin." With half truths from Satan in the Unbeliever's ears, a Teacher's words can come across as mere talk. An Unbeliever can easily assume the Teacher is expressing a religious opinion and some interesting ideas but not the truth of God.

When a Wanderer or a Wonderer meets an Imparter, amazing experiences can happen: healing, prophecy, words of knowledge. Those forms of ministry can have a powerful influence on both the Wanderer and the Wonderer. But when God moves in a supernatural way, Satan responds with two attacks. First, he tells the Unbeliever that what happened was unexplainable, so they were just lucky to be there to see it. If they agree with that lie, they'll eventually store the miraculous event under the "that was cool" label. The second thing Satan tells them is that it wasn't just God doing it; it was also the Imparter. "He has real power." Then Satan will suggest the Unbeliever should worship the Imparter and forget about God. Both are lies, as we know. But when an Unbeliever entertains the lies, they bring confusion and reduce the most dynamic moment of ministry to the status of an interesting coincidence.

I offer this explanation of the typical outcomes for the Wanderer and the Wonderer for two reasons. One is so you will understand that you can approach the Wanderer and the Wonderer with the excitement of a new Believer, the great teaching of an accomplished Teacher, or an amazing impartation of the Holy Spirit, as in the life of the Imparter. All of these are good. But the greatest influence for lifelong change in the life of an Unbeliever comes from the life, love, and devotion of an Example. Showing Christ's love to Unbelievers, even though they don't fully understand what it is, speaks to them more than the excitement of new faith or even miracles. An Example will befriend a person who doesn't have the same moral convictions, loving that person as Christ loves him—and without judging. The Example knows how to be a true friend without compromising his own beliefs or his love and devotion for Jesus. That is a real witness.

The second reason I want to explain the various effects on the Unbeliever is for the benefit of Teachers and Imparters. God has called you to be who you are. But never forget that being an Example of love will have a greater effect on Unbelievers than your greatest sermon or your most supernatural moment. Never forget to first be an Example to the Wanderer and the Wonderer.

In each stage of growth, a person will have the greatest effect on those who are two stages behind. Those who are Examples have the greatest potential for moving Unbelievers up to become Believers. A Teacher's wisdom works best with Believers, to help them grow into Examples. The Imparter ordains, blesses, and anoints the Examples. Imparters give Examples a God experience that they can share openly with others, moving them to become Teachers.

The next question is this: who pulls the Teacher up to the Imparter stage? That happens only by the choice and work of the Holy Spirit. Yahweh Himself calls Teachers to walk in the gift of the Imparter. It's part of His orderly plan for our lives and for His Kingdom. All you have to say is yes to His plan at each stage.

UNBELIEVERS WHO IMITATE THE TRAPPINGS
OF RIGHTEOUSNESS

God's plan is perfect, and it rests in perfect order. When it comes to the five stages of spiritual growth, there are no set times by which you must move forward to the next stage. But a great hole is created when you skip a stage. What happens when you try to go from a Wonderer to an Example, skipping the Believer stage? This is very similar to a high school student who decides that, through personal effort and willpower, he will remain a virgin until he's married. He doesn't make this commitment in obedience to Christ or because the Holy Spirit showed him that God desires His children to reserve sex for marriage. Instead, this kid decides to remain a virgin as a test of his will, or to please his parents, or to be thought of as a good guy. Or maybe he feels it is the most healthy option.

This kid could be an active church member, or it's possible he *never* has been inside a church. Either way, he's an Unbeliever who wants to be moral. After some time passes, he is faced with a powerful temptation—perhaps when he leaves home for college. Faced with all that temptation, he becomes sexually active. He can rationalize his behavior without much trouble. "This girl is probably my future spouse," he will tell himself. Or possibly, "I'd been wondering what it was like to have sex, so I went ahead and tried it."

This young man is still an Unbeliever, but for a long time he has been masquerading as a Believer. Wanderers and Wonderers who try to live like a Christian without first accepting the salvation that Christ offers will never last. When a person tries to skip the Believer stage and rush ahead to live like an Example, the effort is doomed to failure.

You must first grow through the stage of Believer so you can learn to love and obey Christ. Only then can you move ahead and sustain the obedient life of an Example. Time always shows what a person really lives for: self or God. Without becoming a Believer, it is impossible to live for God.

The same thing happens to many adults who are Unbelievers. I've been around some of the most generous, loving Wanderers and Wonderers in the country. I'm amazed at the time and money they give to the needy and underprivileged. Unbelievers often do things out of love for others. They have a genuine desire to help people, not just a desire to make it appear to others that they are generous. They do good things and help large numbers of people. However, they have no spiritual motivation to do these things. They just know that it seems like the right thing to do.

And I have seen a shift in these people over time. They move from doing things out of love, which is a great motivation, to doing it for more personal reasons. They like how it makes them feel, or they find they can use the platform that it gives them to raise their name higher among others. They become known for supporting a particular charitable cause, and it helps their career or their standing in the community. After a while they are motivated to continue helping others because it does so much to advance their personal agenda.

BELIEVERS WHO RUSH AHEAD

Trying to go from Believer to Teacher while skipping the lessons learned as an Example is dangerous, both for you and for those you teach. The crucial lessons you avoid by skipping the Example stage and the issues that go unaddressed will slant your teaching away from a simple and straightforward proclamation of the gospel. You will teach primarily from your unaddressed issues instead of from the Word of God. By attempting to explain a life you yourself are not living, you open the door for error. You also set yourself up for a fall, one that endangers you and those you are attempting to instruct.

Many great Teachers of the gospel have fallen, and it always seems to come out of nowhere. Actually, all great falls started long before the news media picked up on the story. They began when the Teacher skipped over being an Example in one or more parts of his or her life. That lack of order created a hole. Satan knew it and waited for the most destructive time to step through it, and then he destroyed the person's ministry.

Likewise, problems arise when a Christian rushes ahead from Example to Imparter, skipping over the Teacher stage. Such a person who tries to do the ministry of the Imparter is usually working and living in isolation. Because they are not pouring their lives into others as Teachers, they get to the point where they become "lone Christians." When Examples attempt to carry out the ministry of impartation without first growing through the Teacher stage, they miss many of the lessons God wants to teach them. There will be a hole in his or her walk.

When God anoints a Teacher with the gift of impartation, through orderly spiritual growth, that Teacher is already surrounded by students. The lessons learned in the Teacher stage position the Teacher to use the impartation gift in orderly ways.

Everyone needs people from each of the five stages in their life. Everyone needs to live in relationship with an Unbeliever, a Believer, an Example, a Teacher, and an Imparter. Doing that keeps you accountable to each level and keeps you in the right order. If you keep your progression in order, each stage will show you the perfect will of God and prepare you for the stage to come.

CHAPTER 18

The Year God Gave Me Nine Cities

We mentor young men to change the world.

—FROM THE MOTTO OF THE SHAUN ALEXANDER FOUNDATION

In my NFL career, after I was released by the Seattle Seahawks, the Washington Redskins signed me for a season. As a result, I moved my family from Seattle and purchased a home on the outskirts of Washington DC.

It was an exciting time for us. We were living in a new house in a new area, and our fourth child was due in a short time. But even with all the excitement of the coming baby, it was an odd time. We were no longer living in Seattle, and I wasn't in the play-offs, as I had been the previous five years. It also had been a year of intense praying for direction—every day, early in the morning. The Holy Spirit was still in me and on me in a powerful way. I was growing in it and loving every moment of it.

One afternoon in January 2009, I was in my office, praying. I had been asking the Holy Spirit about loyalty and forgiveness: what it looked like and how to live a life defined by forgiving others. While I was praying, I heard God whisper, *You are going to speak in nine cities from January to July.*

At first I laughed and thought, *I must have just imagined that, because there is no way Valerie is going to be cool with that.* She was due the following month. I receive numerous offers to speak, but I don't accept them unless Valerie and I both feel God is telling us I should go. God is a God of order, so I know He would never have Valerie and me be in disagreement about whether I should accept a speaking invitation. When we do disagree, I don't make a decision until God gives us both the same answer.

The next day I was sitting in my office, and I received a nudge that people from the nine cities were about to start calling with invitations. I had been studying and learning about obedience at each level of spiritual maturity. So in response to what I heard from God, I went to find Valerie. I told her, "Babe, I think God is about to have me speak a lot this offseason, like nine cities."

She looked at me and smiled. "I knew God was going to do something with you soon."

That's what I mean. When God is moving in your life, things have order. The same God who spoke to me about what was going to happen also spoke to my wife about it. And we both heard His voice and responded.

GOD'S ORDER IN YOUR LIFE

Later that day Judah Smith called. Judah was the youth pastor of the City Church in Kirkland, Washington, near Seattle. His youth ministry was called Generation Church. When I lived in Kirkland, I used to hang out with Judah and Generation Church even though it was not the church I regularly attended. We are good friends, and we talk often about life and our families. That day, as we were about to end our conversation, Judah invited me to speak at the Generation Church Conference. It was scheduled for March, and I knew then that Kirkland was one of the nine cities.

Over the next ten days I agreed to speak in nine cities, including

Baton Rouge, Kirkland-Seattle, Los Angeles, Tulsa, Washington DC, Atlanta, Dallas, Mobile, and Birmingham. In some of the cities I would speak more than once. I was excited to see how quickly it came together, but I had no idea what was about to take place.

During the previous off-season, when I was released from the Seattle Seahawks, God took my prayer life to that new "in me and on me" level I described in chapter 1. During that time the Holy Spirit led me to take a deep look at the young men I was pouring my life into. I began to pay more attention to how much time I spent with each man and the things God was giving me to teach each one. I began to understand a little more why Jesus had only twelve disciples. I noticed the ways they were a little more special to Jesus than the masses who also responded to Him.

As I prepared for the nine-city journey, God whispered to me again. You are going to take your closest thirteen disciples with you to the nine cities. They will all grow in ways that they never would have dreamed. They will see signs and wonders. Some of them will use the gifts of the Holy Spirit for the first time.

I asked God, "Who are my thirteen?" Then I started to write down the names of the ones I thought were supposed to go on this journey: Andrew, Shep, Brian, Kyle, Jordan, Vince… God stopped me and said, *Shaun, ten of your thirteen are correct. Three are not, and you will know which three as it happens. But tell the ten to count the costs.*

All the men I disciple and mentor are important to me, and I love them all like my real brothers. But I understood that the nine-city journey was a mission from God and the right thirteen men better be with me. As I thought about the men I was mentoring and discipling, I realized they were as different from one another as night and day. Some grew up in Christian homes; some didn't. Some were wild; some weren't. I met some in high school and some in college. Choosing the correct ones was crucial to what God had in mind for us.

A few days later I was talking to my brother Durran about what was happening and how God was taking me on this nine-city journey. We talked about the power of the Scriptures.

Durran said, "Isn't it amazing how perfect and authentic the gospels are. The only thing different about Matthew, Mark, Luke, and John is how they related the story from their point of view." Then he said, "Think about it. If we were watching something happen outside, we would tell the same story, but it would still be a little different from our own points of view."

That conversation got me to thinking about how important it is to remember and preserve a record of what God does in your life. The memories of the disciples' experiences with Jesus formed the basis for their accounts of His life. What they wrote about Him still affects lives today.

As I got off the phone, I felt God nudging me again. *As you go through the trips, have the boys all write down what happens. I want this to be authentic.*

When I picked the first ten to join me, I called them in pairs and explained what was happening. I asked them to pick which of the nine cities they would want to come to. I figured I'd bring along at least one man, but would try to bring three or four, to each city. I told them to start praying about what God wanted them to see and how they were supposed to mature during this time. Order is important, and that order applied to the nine-city journey.

By the end of January, the ten men—Andrew, Shep, Brian, Kyle, Jordan, Vince, Marco, Trevor, Dayton, and Derek—were selected. I was reading through the book of Acts again and suggested they should too. I was excited about the prospect that some ordinary, unschooled men, very much like Peter and John, would walk with such an anointing that everyone they met would acknowledge there was something special about the God they served. The people who met the original disciples either followed Jesus or hardened their hearts and refused. Either way, the walk of those twelve men brought a decisive response from the people they encountered. That became my goal for me and the men who would travel with me on the nine-city journey. We would walk in such a way that our walk would make people want to make a real decision for Jesus, not by our force, but by the power and love of Christ.

GOD'S VOICE DOESN'T DEPEND ON YOUR FEELINGS

The nine-city journey started in Mobile, Alabama. Our trip there coincided with my induction into the Senior Bowl Hall of Fame.[1] The induction ceremony was held on Friday night prior to the Senior Bowl game the following day.

Ronnie Cottrell, who was one of my coaches when I played at the University of Alabama, was now the head coach at Alma Bryant High School. The school is located in Bayou La Batre, near Mobile. Coach Cottrell had a vision to reach the city of Mobile and the surrounding area for Christ. Sunday morning my mother and father, my brother Durran, and two of my young men (Jordan and Dayton) went with Coach Cottrell and me to a church in Bayou La Batre. There we announced that God had called us to visit nine cities. In those cities many would find salvation, restoration, and supernatural intervention in their lives.

As we were leaving the hotel to go to the church, I grabbed my camcorder. I looked at the men who had come with me and said, "How amazing would it have been if the disciples had carried a camcorder with them when they were walking with Jesus? Think about what we would have seen if Paul or Barnabas had taken a camcorder along on their missions. We are going to film everything."

None of them had walked in the supernatural before. None of them had been hit by the wave of prophetic ministry that only God can pour out. It was all ahead of us and about to start, sooner than we realized.

When the church service in Bayou La Batre ended, the pastor told the congregation that anyone wanting prayer should come down front where we were standing. Many people responded, some with a word of encouragement for us. Others came to confess sin in their life. Then I saw this big kid. *He has to be a football player*, I thought, so I asked him.

"I play but not like I want to," he replied. "I have a bad back."

It's a tough thing for a boy that size to be unable to play high school football. So I asked, "Has anybody prayed for your back to be healed?"

"No," he replied.

He was like most young men in the South who have grown up in the church. He could pray, but it was really just a formality. I know because I was like that once.

Jordan and Dayton came over and put their hands on his shoulders. I walked behind him and put my hands on his back. After a moment I prayed, but I didn't feel anything. From the time God had begun to move in me and on me in the early-morning prayer time, I had always sensed God's presence. If I didn't feel that same sensation, I assumed either something was wrong or God wasn't completely present. I was about to learn how wrong I was.

I looked at the high school kid and asked, "How do you feel?"

He said, "Good, I guess."

"What about your back?" When I first saw him at the front of the church, all I knew was that I was supposed to pray for him. I didn't know what to expect from the prayer. So I waited for his response. The kid gave me a questioning look and remained silent.

"How's your back?" I asked again.

He laughed. "I'm not sure. It always feels fine when I'm standing up. It's when I sit down that I feel the pain."

"Well, sit down and stand back up," I said. He sat down, and when he stood up, a smile came across his face.

"Do it again," I said. He sat down and stood up again.

"Nothing," he said. "I feel nothing." He laughed again. "I can't explain it, but all the pain is gone."

As he walked away, I was thinking about the fact that I hadn't felt anything while I was praying for him. God whispered to me, Shaun, I'm not just a tingly feeling. I'm more than just a good touch. Don't trust how it feels to you, and don't trust your emotions. Trust only My voice and My Word. Do what I say, when I say, and things will happen that you have never seen before.

I had a feeling that this would be the start of something I would never want to end. "God, whatever You say, I will do." Let the nine-city journey begin.

CHAPTER 19

God Does the Unthinkable Through the Unqualified

I have become all things to all men so that
by all possible means I might save some.
—PAUL, THE APOSTLE (1 CORINTHIANS 9:22)

W hen I began writing this chapter, I wanted to tell about all nine cities that we visited and why they were special. But that would fill a couple of books. So I will tell you something that happened in three of the cities. Every time I watch the videos we made, I become more in awe of who God is and how He demonstrates His power and might.

The God we follow is the same God who told Noah to build a boat because He was going to make it rain, even though it never had rained before. The same God who walked in the furnace with Shadrach, Meshach, and Abednego, and none of them was burned by the fire. The same God who knocked Saul to the ground and asked him, "Why do you persecute me?" The same God, the great I Am, Yahweh, the One who is, was, and is to come.

A few weeks after our trip to Mobile, I was in Washington DC for the National Prayer Breakfast. There I met Emmanuel from Dallas, number eleven of the thirteen men who would accompany me in two more cities. In March I went to Baton Rouge, Louisiana, for a men's conference at Healing Place Church. About eight hundred men were there, worshiping Jesus and growing together. It was a powerful sight. The pastor at Healing Place is a very good man named Dino Rizzo. On that trip I brought along Andrew from Seattle, Vince from West Palm Beach, and Dayton from Birmingham.

When we arrived, we went to our rooms and spent time praying for the service that night and for the entire conference. An hour later someone picked us up and drove us to the church. I wasn't scheduled to speak until the next day, so that night we just soaked up the atmosphere. The music started, and people began to worship. That's when Dayton tapped me on the shoulder and asked, "Who's the main pastor?"

Funny thing was I didn't know which of the men was Dino Rizzo. We looked around and tried to guess, but none of us could figure it out. After we had sung several worship songs, a man who had been on his knees worshiping near the front of the audience got up and walked in our direction. I thought, *Is that Dino?* As he got closer, I knew it was.

"Hey, Shaun," he said with a smile. "Glad you're here." He walked past me and up the steps and grabbed the microphone.

Wow! He was the pastor. He'd been praying hard and worshiping hard, like he was desperate for God to answer his prayers. That was a powerful moment. The spirit of Dino and the Healing Place Church made us know that the Spirit of God flowed in that place. I was excited about speaking there and eager to see what might happen.

The next day I told the men at the conference a story about the time the pope drove his own car and got pulled over for running a light. He had a new driver who was nervous about working his first day on the job, so the pope said to the driver, "I think I'll get behind the wheel."

The driver knew this wasn't normal, and he wondered if the pope had ever driven a car before. He politely told the pope, "Your Holiness, I will be glad to drive you anywhere you wish to go."

The pope responded very gently, "I haven't driven in a long time. I'll go just a few blocks, then I'll get in the back, and you can drive." Then the pope grabbed the driver's arm and said, "My son, are you going to tell the pope no?"

Reluctantly the driver handed the keys to the pope and took a seat in the back of the limo. The pope was getting excited as he climbed behind the wheel and started off. When they had driven a few blocks and reached the first stop sign, the pope glanced back at the driver, then pressed the gas pedal and drove through the intersection.

Down the block he came to a traffic light, and as he approached, it turned to yellow. He thought, *Maybe I should slow down,* but something came over him. The pope shoved the gas pedal to the floor and shot through the intersection. Seconds later a police car came up behind them, lights flashing and siren screaming. The pope pulled over and waited.

The officer walked up to the car, looked inside, and did a double take. Then he slowly backed away, gave the limo a once-over, and walked back to his police cruiser. His partner asked him, "What are you doing? You didn't give them a ticket."

The first policeman, still dazed, gave no answer.

His partner looked at him again. "Whose car is that, anyway?"

The first policeman looked at his partner and said, "I don't know whose car it is, but the pope is driving him."

WHAT GOD'S ANOINTING LOOKS LIKE

That evening I went on to teach about how we have a misconception about serving God and what it looks like. We aren't clear about what

God's followers look like, act like, and live like. We fall for the lie that if we are good guys, attend church, and live moral lives, we will go to heaven when we die. I spoke for almost an hour, and when I finished, more than one hundred men came to the front to give their lives to Jesus.

As I was walking off the stage, I felt God say to me, *Is that all you came here to do?*

I walked back to the microphone and said, "I know I'm supposed to pray for people today, so if you need prayer, I'll be up front."

The response was almost overwhelming. So many people responded that I wasn't sure how to handle them. But Dino knew what to do. He took Vince, Dayton, Andrew, and me to a prayer room. One by one, men came in for prayer. God's presence in that room was thick and tangible. After fifteen minutes of praying for people, it became even more intense. Guys would enter the room, and almost as soon as they arrived, the Holy Spirit would tell me what they were going through, what they needed, and how to minister to them. They would start to speak, and I would stop them. "Don't say anything." Then I would tell them what the Holy Spirit was telling me about them. Some of them came into the room, and without anyone saying anything, they burst into tears.

After about an hour I was praying for a man, and the Holy Spirit said, *Ask Andrew and Dayton what I just told them about this next guy.* So when the next man came into the room, I looked over at Andrew and said, "What are you thinking?" Andrew told the man about his job and the people around him. Then he told the guy about the drugs the guy was using with his buddies. The guy looked like he had seen a ghost. He repented right there, and we prayed for him.

Two guys later, I asked Dayton to tell me what he heard. He asked the man about his daughter. The man's eyes started to tear up. "I'm not from here; I'm from Texas. I was just driving by, and something told me to come in here, so I did. I heard you speak and was about to leave. Then something said to get in line and see you. My daughter is sick, and I'm so far away from her. I just need someone to talk to about it. I need someone to help me give it to God." He cried so hard. All I did was hug him.

It was exciting to see God's hand on us. For some of the men that night, the word they received called them out, pointing out hidden sin in their lives and letting them know God sees it all. For others it was a message as simple as "I am here with you." But in every instance, it was a powerful and amazing experience. We prayed and ministered to people for a little more than two hours.

As we were leaving the building, one of the people helping with the conference pulled me aside. He told me that he knew most of the people who had come in the room for prayer. He said he had never seen a group of young men tell so many people, young and old, sick and healthy, about their lives and be consistently right. We were only beginning our nine-city journey, and already we had seen a great prophetic anointing poured out on us.

THE SEATTLE EXPERIENCE

Two weeks later we flew out to Seattle to see Judah Smith and Generation Church. I took with me Shep, who was twenty-five, working for the Fellowship of Christian Athletes (FCA), and living in Atlanta. I had met him ten years earlier at an FCA camp when he was fifteen and living in Orlando, Florida. With him was Jordan, from Wisconsin, who was twenty-one and a college student. Also joining us were Derek, age twenty-four, from Portland, Oregon (whom I met and began to disciple in training camp when we played for the Seattle Seahawks), and Andrew, who had been with me earlier.

In Seattle we all stayed at my old house. Some of the guys from the church I attended when my family lived out there came by the house too.

They had been in high school back then; now they were in college. That first night we caught up on one another's lives, then we attended the opening session of the conference. I wasn't scheduled to speak until the next afternoon.

When I woke up the following morning, God started asking me questions about humility. *Would you give the microphone to one of the young men with you if I told you to?* My answer was, "Yes. Of course."

After I asked God four times whether He was serious about it, I knew what I was going to do. When it came time for me to speak, they introduced me to the crowd. I spoke for about ten minutes, then introduced Shep. For the next hour he told the audience how he had found God's grace at the FCA camp and learned to walk out that faith in his daily life. Seeing him there and knowing what he'd come through left me amazed at how God had worked through both of us to bring that moment together. Shep's testimony was anointed and powerful.

As I came back to the podium with tears in my eyes, I explained salvation to the young people in the audience. I told them it was Jesus asking them to go all-in with Him. More than one hundred youth came up front to go all-in with Jesus. As they moved away from the front for prayer and other ministry, I started talking about Peter's shadow and Paul's handkerchiefs. I explained that the Holy Spirit was on those men so completely that God would work wonders even when people had contact only with Peter's shadow or when they would touch something of Paul's (see Acts 5:15; 19:11–12).

I sensed that God wanted to do more ministry than the call for salvation, so I joined my guys on the floor, and we walked down the aisles. As we made our way through the crowd, I reached over and touched various ones, ministering, praying, and sharing a prophetic word.

The next day people came up to me and said, "Wow, your words really impacted me. You are an amazing teacher. Thanks for sharing yesterday." I thanked them, but I remembered a scripture from the gospel of John: "The Pharisees heard that Jesus was gaining and baptizing more disciples than John, although in fact it was not Jesus who baptized, but his disciples" (John 4:1–2).

The crowd hadn't responded to me; they had responded to what God said through Shep. When you listen to God, the right person speaks, and the right person hears.

THE REDEMPTIVE POWER OF PROPHECY

In April I spoke at meetings in Tulsa, Washington DC, and Atlanta. I took different ones with me of the thirteen guys. While I was in Washington DC, I spoke at the National Community Church. The church meets in three movie theaters and at a coffeehouse. Their senior pastor, Mark Batterson, has a great heart and a simple solution to everything: "Be extreme when loving God and people." While at his church I found my twelfth guy, a young college graduate named Jon. He accompanied us to three of the nine cities; one of them was a trip to Los Angeles.

In Los Angeles we visited the Dream Center. Along with Jon, I brought Trevor, who was raised in Seattle but lives in Austin, Texas, and Derek from Portland and Marco from San Diego. For this trip several of us brought guests. Jon brought Joel, one of the National Community Church pastors. Derek brought Curtis, one of his closest friends, who played football in junior college with Derek but now lives in Los Angeles. Marco brought a young man named Jake, whom he discipled. Trevor didn't bring anyone, but I brought two guests: David, who went to college in Los Angeles, and my cousin Quincy, who lived in northern California.

The night we arrived in Los Angeles, we discussed what we would do during the next two days. After a while the conversations separated us into smaller groups. Later on I gathered everyone for prayer. As we prayed, the Holy Spirit began to move. Jon was caught up in the Spirit and went around the group giving a prophetic word to each one of us. The guys were amazed, but no one was more amazed than Jon. He told Quincy so many things about Quincy's life that he started admitting hidden sin.

The next morning we rode over to the Dream Center to help with their ministry to feed the poor and the homeless. Marco was reading 1 Corinthians, and he tapped me on the leg. "Look at this." He pointed to a passage:

> If an unbeliever or someone who does not understand comes in while everybody is prophesying, he will be convinced by all that he is a sinner and will be judged by all, and the secrets of his heart will be laid bare. So he will fall down and worship God, exclaiming, "God is really among you!" (1 Corinthians 14:24–25)

Marco was excited. "This is what happened last night. We were prophesying. Quincy got convicted and started telling us about his trouble." Then he threw back his head and screamed, "God is here! God is really here!"

The rest of the trip was amazing. I could tell you about the people who lived in the Dream Center, the projects that we visited to pass out food, the worship at Angelus Temple, or even the overflow of prayer afterward, where we saw a kid on a stretcher. He couldn't move anything except his eyes, but we prayed for him, and he moved his hands and feet and turned his head.

Instead I will tell you this: God is amazing, and He is still doing the unthinkable with the unqualified.

The nine-city journey was as much for me as it was for the guys I took along or the people to whom we ministered. Through that journey

I had the opportunity to experience what I've been praying about and
talking about:

- God's order and how we are empowered through His order
- God's powerful, healing, and prophetic presence
- How God is made tangibly real in the lives of people through
  us, His servants

God used our experiences on the nine-city journey to bring the power
of the Imparter to a new level in my life. We saw more than one thousand
people confess that Jesus is Lord and Savior. And He taught me the power
of discipleship. But you'll have to wait for another book to hear all about
that.

CHAPTER 20

The Walk
to Spiritual Maturity

> It has given me great joy to find some
> of your children walking in the truth,
> just as the Father commanded us.
>
> —JOHN, THE APOSTLE (2 JOHN 4)

The steps to spiritual maturity follow an orderly process from Unbeliever (Wanderer and Wonderer) to Believer to Example to Teacher to Imparter. That order is evident in the lives of the great men and women of the Bible. In this book we have followed that progression by studying Peter's life, but it is easily recognizable in the lives of other biblical figures.

Moses was a Wonderer in Pharaoh's court, wondering who he was and what it meant that he was a Hebrew, but not really believing much of anything. He became a Believer, but his lack of understanding put him in a difficult position. As a member of Pharaoh's court, he had great freedom, but as a Hebrew who was newly aware of his spiritual heritage, he wanted to identify with his own people. When Moses saw an Egyptian beating one of the Hebrew slaves, he struck the man and killed him. Because of that, he fled to the wilderness. There Moses learned what it meant to believe in God and became rooted and grounded in the Hebrew faith. Working through that changed his life and made him an Example.

As an Example, Moses returned to Egypt and appeared before Pharaoh, arguing for the release of the Hebrew slaves. By the time Pharaoh agreed to let them leave, Moses was a Teacher and on the verge of becoming an Imparter.

Moses and the slaves left Egypt bound for the Promised Land. Not long after they left their captors, Pharaoh sent his army to bring them back. With the Egyptian army quickly closing in, Moses stood with the people of God on the banks of the Red Sea, raised his staff, and watched as God opened a way through the water. The Hebrews crossed to the opposite side on dry ground, and Moses the Teacher became Moses the Imparter. The sea came back together and swallowed the pursuing Egyptian army.

GOD'S ORDER IN THE LIFE OF PAUL

Paul followed much the same progression. A devout Jew, he sought the Messiah but did not believe Jesus was He. Paul was a Wanderer who persecuted Christians, but he became a Believer on the road to Damascus. Following his conversion, he spent time in the desert alone, figuring out what it meant to follow Christ. Afterward, he submitted his understanding to Peter and the other apostles in Jerusalem, then he went off to Antioch as an Example. In Antioch, he grew from Example to Teacher. When he left on his first missionary journey, he was still a Teacher, but he returned an Imparter and remained one until his death. God worked His wonders through Paul the apostle.

Jesus promised the disciples that after He ascended to heaven, God would send the Comforter, God's Spirit, to be with them and in them. When Peter preached in Jerusalem after the Spirit descended at Pentecost, he told the crowd that what they were seeing and experiencing was the outpouring of the Holy Spirit foretold by the prophet Joel. Jews and Christians of the first century were witnessing the day when young men and women would prophesy, old men would dream dreams, young men would see visions. This was a time when there would be wonders in heaven and people would experience signs on earth. That outpouring of the Holy Spirit at Pentecost opened the way for Believers to enter into power and ministry like that of the apostles and the prophets of old.

There is an order to God's work in our lives, with very few exceptions. God determines how fast we progress and how far we go, but a disciple's walk always takes him or her through the orderly steps: Unbeliever, Believer, Example, Teacher, Imparter. Some people move through those stages slowly; some move rather quickly.

When I was in high school, one of my closest friends was a guy named Ray. He was the wildest guy in our group, always living on the aggressive edge and pushing the limits. If there was an edge, Ray's first impulse was to go past it. In that respect we were complete opposites and an unlikely pair, but he was one of my best friends.

I left Florence, Kentucky, for the University of Alabama after high school. The Seattle Seahawks drafted me in April 2000, following my final season at Alabama. I moved to Seattle in May to begin training and working out with the team. I met Valerie, my soul mate who eventually became my wife, the first day I got there.

Meanwhile Ray was living in Florence. By then he had graduated from Western Kentucky University and was working at a bank. It was getting close to the end of July, and my first training camp was about to start in Seattle. Ray, my brother Durran, Josh, and some of my closest friends decided to take me to Kings Island, an amusement park in Cincinnati, to have our last time together before the NFL season started and I moved across the country for good.

As Ray and I stood in line for one of the roller coasters, he started asking me about my life in Seattle and what it was like in the NFL. I told him that we spent a lot of time studying game films. Lifting and running were intense, but the amount of time we spent studying game plans and plays and the opposing teams was unbelievable.

I asked him what he was doing, and he said, "You know. Working the nine to five." I could tell he wasn't feeling too enthusiastic about it.

"Back to you," Ray said. "There is not that much film in the world, and I know you, Shaun. What do *you* do in Seattle?"

He was right. I never was consumed by any one thing. I thought about his question, and all I could think about was Valerie. I started telling him about her. Ray grinned. "I have never heard you talk about a girl like this before." He shook his head and looked at the ground in silence. I had never thought about it until Ray asked me, but in Seattle if I wasn't practicing or working out, I was either with Valerie or trying to find a way to be with her.

Finally Ray broke the silence. "I'm through with this world. Everything you touch turns out good. Your life is full: full of joy, full of people, full of life. I've tried everything, and I'm empty."

We left Kings Island, and two days later I boarded a flight to Seattle. That night Ray went to a party. While he was there, he said to God, "If You are real, fill this emptiness I feel inside of me." Ray said no to drugs for the first time in his life. The next Sunday he gave his heart to Jesus and joined the church. He became involved with classes and Bible studies and poured himself into it. God moved in a tremendous way, opening Ray's heart and spirit to teaching and spiritual growth.

After six months of watching God move in the lives of others, Ray answered a calling. He quit his job at the bank and became a youth pastor. A month after that he took the youth group on a mission trip to

Africa. There he stepped into the fullness of the Holy Spirit. While on that trip, Ray took his youth group into a home for people who were helpless. There he prayed for a blind man, and the blind man's eyes popped open.

OBEYING GOD'S DIRECTION AND TIMING

There is no limit to what God can do in your life, but you have to accept His direction and His timing. Regardless of the pace, everyone who ministers from the fullness of the Holy Spirit works through each level of maturity in the same sequence. That is God's order for your maturity in Christ. It is essential to follow that process. The effectiveness of your growth and ministry in each succeeding stage depends on the thoroughness you achieved in the previous stage. Those who try to skip a step or rush through a stage do so at the risk of injury to themselves and others.

We've all seen and read news accounts of pastors who had a meteoric rise from obscurity to become head of a large congregation, only to be trapped in a scandal. Then they fall to the bottom. Anyone can fall at any level and for any number of reasons. But most of the time the problem comes from trying to skip the lessons of one stage in order to reach the next stage too quickly. Taking a shortcut allows error to creep into your theology, practice, and lifestyle.

Jesus lived thirty-three years on earth. He spent the first thirty years preparing to disciple twelve men. Only the last three years were spent actually doing the work of ministry. Moses spent forty years in Pharaoh's court and forty years in the wilderness. So for eighty years, in some way he was preparing to spend the last forty years of his life as the leader of the Hebrews.

God takes a long view of human history and a long view of your life. He's more interested in your character than in how fast you can become a successful minister, lawyer, doctor, entertainer, or whatever occupation He leads you to pursue. He's not out to make you a success at anything other than a success at hearing His voice, knowing His name, and doing His will. The steps I've outlined in *The Walk* are the way in which God works in your life, beginning when you don't yet know Him.

So learn God's order, love God's order, and live God's order! If you do, He will use you in ways you would never imagine.

Living in God's Order

Form a Group and Get More from The Walk

The most important question anyone can ask has to do with God and how He works in our lives. How does God reveal His will? How can you know you are hearing God's voice and not simply your own desires? How does God want to work through His followers in His Kingdom? What is the best way to keep growing in Christlikeness?

In this seven-session study, you will explore God's work in the lives of biblical characters and in your own life. The study is designed to be used in a small-group setting. The teachings are applicable to men, women, college students, teenagers, parents, singles, clergy, laypersons, and spiritual seekers. Even two friends or a couple who want to discuss the life of faith will find this discussion guide helpful.

The guide is organized around the five stages of spiritual maturity. The questions are designed to encourage open discussion without putting anyone on the spot. The goal is not to come up with the perfect answer but to explore God's work as He leads you in spiritual growth and maturity.

In *The Walk*, Shaun Alexander suggests that Christians today can have the same kind of power and ministry as the prophets of old and the first-century believers. This guide will help you make God's work personal in your own life.

SESSION 1: YOUR PERSONAL INTRODUCTION TO THE WALK

In the Bible we see that God works in people's lives in a certain order, starting before they even commit their lives to Christ. He does the same thing today. In each of the five stages of spiritual maturity, God teaches us and trains us in faith, obedience, love, service, and taking on the character of Christ. And as we grow in spiritual maturity, we also grow in the experience of God's Spirit being "in us and on us."

God will grow your faith, shape your character, and use you in ministry in ways that you never dreamed were possible. Shaun began studying the order of God's work in our lives at a time when he was injured and forced to sit out most of a season in the National Football League. At first it didn't look like a positive development, but it grew to influence his entire approach to ministry.

For Discussion

1. In the book's introduction, Shaun points out the importance of not dragging your feet and also not trying to run ahead of God, but to walk *with* God. Why is it important to allow God to set the pace for your life without trying to speed up or slow down His work?

2. God's work in our lives is not haphazard or random. Shaun cites 1 Corinthians 14:33: "For God is not a God of disorder but of peace." (Also, read 1 Corinthians 14:40.) God leads people through an identifiable sequence of five stages of growth, starting with Unbeliever and ending with Imparter. How have you seen God bring order to your life? Tell about a time of confusion or personal chaos when you asked God to give you clear direction and a sense of purpose.

3. Discuss characters from the Bible whose lives showed evidence of God's leading them and teaching them through stages of spiritual maturity. (Examples include Peter, Moses, Paul, and Elisha.) Can you think of incidents from Scripture that reveal God's order in other areas beyond personal spiritual growth? How would you have responded to the things these Bible characters experienced?

4. Tell about a person you know whose life is changing right before your eyes. What event started that person's transformation? How do you think you would respond if a similar life-changing event took place in your life?

5. It's easy to think of adversity as a negative thing. Trials and difficulties are uncomfortable, but frequently they are the circumstances that God uses to redirect our lives. For Shaun, an injury took him away from football, but it became a doorway into the next phase of his life. What trouble or difficulty have you experienced recently? How is God using that trial to give you new direction?

6. Shaun heard the Holy Spirit tell him to start waking up early every morning to meet with God for a time of prayer and study. It wasn't a call to a long list of spiritual disciplines—just one. What is one new spiritual discipline you could practice for the next thirty days? Ask God to show you His will in this area.

7. Even from a young age, Shaun wanted to see God work through him in the same way God had worked through the great men and women in the Bible. What is your vision for your life with God? How is He already working through you? What would you like to become as you grow in Christ?

8. Shaun describes the experience of the fullness of Christ as the Holy Spirit being "in you and on you." Jesus promised His

disciples much the same when He told them He would send
His Spirit, "for he lives with you and will be in you" (John
14:17). Have you ever sensed the Holy Spirit's presence in your
life like that? If so, tell the group about it.

SESSION 2: THE UNBELIEVER (THE WANDERER AND THE WONDERER)

Everyone begins the Walk as an Unbeliever. Wanderers go through life with
no sense of ultimate purpose. They might be aware that others are seeking
meaning and purpose in life, but those are not the questions that motivate
a Wanderer. On the other hand, Wonderers do have questions about meaning and purpose, but they don't know where to find the answers.

For Discussion

1. Shaun suggests that a Wanderer is like dandelion seeds blown
   randomly by the wind. Meanwhile, a Wonderer is like a young
   child who plays a game the same way every time and keeps
   wondering why the outcome never changes. "Whatever she
   does, she still gets the same result. She knows something is not
   complete, and she wants more out of the game, but she has no
   answers." If you are not a Believer, do you identify with either
   description? Why or why not? If you are a Believer, would you
   describe your past life as either a Wanderer or a Wonderer?
   Why or why not?

2. The stage of being an Unbeliever has its own trials, traps, and
   victories. The traps often carry serious consequences. Think
   back to some of the traps you got caught in as an Unbeliever.
   What were the consequences? What lasting effect(s) have they
   had on your life?

3. The victory of an Unbeliever comes in finding faith in Christ. That faith includes two essential components. First, believing that Jesus is Lord. And, second, believing that God raised Him from the dead, conquering death and making Jesus the Savior of the world (see Romans 10:9). If you are an Unbeliever, what keeps you from believing that Jesus is the Son of God and your Savior (see John 3:16–18) and the Lord of the universe (see Colossians 1:15–17)?

4. Peter came to a moment in life when he had to decide whether Jesus was Lord. For many of us, that is exactly how the issue arises—through a clear and conscious decision made at a definite point in time. Can you identify a time in your life when you said yes to Christ? If so, share it with the group. Can you think of a time when you said no to Christ? Can you tell the group about the circumstances surrounding that time?

5. God is at work in the lives of Unbelievers who are aware of Him even if they don't currently acknowledge it (see Ecclesiastes 3:11 and Romans 1:20). Christians, of course, have an important role to play in helping Wanderers and Wonderers find God, and the key is through building relationships. Who built a relationship with you and showed you an example of Christ? Who motivated you to become a follower of Jesus? Think of one Unbeliever with whom you can start building a similar relationship.

SESSION 3: THE LIFE OF THE BELIEVER

In chapter 5, Shaun tells the story of tightrope walker Philippe Petit. After crossing a wire between the towers of the World Trade Center, Petit brought out a wheelbarrow and invited onlookers to get in and ride across the wire. This is a vivid illustration of the life of faith. It is not merely mental assent or a statement of belief. It is a full life commitment. As we grow spiritually, God issues the invitation for us to be fully committed in different areas of our lives. As Believers grow, they learn what it means to hand over every attachment, every habit, every plan and ambition, every sin, and every part of their life to God. That is what Shaun means when he talks about being all-in.

For Discussion

1. What has God been pointing out to you recently? What area of your life is He telling you to put "in the wheelbarrow"? Are you struggling to let go of the person, behavior, relationship, attitude, or sin that God wants you to hand over? When you think about this struggle, what person, actions, or attachments prevent you from making that kind of total commitment?

2. We come to Christ through an act of repentance and submission. Repenting of sin and submitting to God's will often begin with a public acknowledgment of our faith in Christ. Have you ever felt God moving you to make your faith known publicly? What are some ways you could share your faith?

3. The life of a Believer has its own trials, traps, and victories. The traps often involve behaviors that a person indulged in as an Unbeliever—behaviors that were outside God's order. Sex, for instance, was created by God to be shared by a husband and wife. It quickly becomes an obsessive trap, however, when couples engage in it outside the boundaries and bonds of marriage. Drugs and alcohol also are common traps. Another trap that is easily overlooked is telling half truths. This can remain a challenge for Believers when they are so concerned about their

image that they tell only part of the truth. They share only what they want others to see about them. Telling only part of the truth serves to make yourself seem better than you are, but it's a trap. What are areas in your life that, as an Unbeliever, you live/lived out of order? Do they remain areas of strong temptation for you now?

4. The Spirit of God lives inside Believers, which gives us access to God's power, wisdom, and victory. Satan cannot remain present when you command him to leave in the name of Jesus Christ. (Read James 4:7; 2 Corinthians 10:4–5; Acts 16:16–18.) Think back to your answer(s) to question 3 regarding areas of habitual temptation. Ask others in your group to pray for you, that you will draw on the power and authority of Christ to defeat Satan when he tempts you.

5. The victories of the Believer stage of spiritual growth come through surrendering to Christ at an ever-deepening level. A major victory is that the character of Christ starts to emerge increasingly in your life. The apostle Paul referred to Christ's character as the fruit of the Holy Spirit. Those elements are listed in Galatians 5:22–23. Read those verses, and discuss which of the characteristics are evident in your life. Which of the attributes of Christ does God want to make more evident in your life?

SESSION 4: THE LIFE OF THE EXAMPLE

An Example is a person who lives out what he or she believes. The life of an Example is a strong witness to an Unbeliever because the Example's life goes beyond words to faithful living and selfless love. As Examples mature in Christ, they provide living proof of the truth of God's Word and the authenticity of His work in a person's life.

For Discussion

1. In chapter 8, Shaun shares that the first step in the growth of an Example is to realize that God is good (see Psalm 34:8). Why is it important to know that God is good? What traps are we able to avoid when we rely on God's goodness? In what ways has God shown His goodness in your life?

2. As we grow spiritually, after goodness we are to add knowledge. And the most important form of knowledge is to know the Scriptures through regular study. (Read 2 Peter 1:5–7.) Do you have a regular time each day that you devote to the study of Scripture? If so, how does it affect your life?

3. We also learn to know the Holy Spirit. His voice is the voice we hear guiding and directing our lives. Have you heard the Holy Spirit speak to you? How do you know the difference between the voice of God's Spirit and your own feelings, ideas, plans, and desires?

4. God uses discipline to train His children in Christlikeness. In the discipline of self-control and perseverance, we find the key to true freedom. Self-control gives you the freedom to become the person you want to become in Christ rather than remaining captive to the traps of the Unbeliever. What areas of your life exhibit self-control?

5. The discipline of perseverance keeps you focused and committed to seeing God work in your life. Perseverance includes the endurance you need to avoid giving in or giving up. What areas of your life present the biggest challenge to your perseverance?

6. Examples are susceptible to the trap of feeling that they always must be perfect. But Jesus didn't call perfect disciples; He called disciples who were willing learners. They kept failing, but they also kept growing in faith, knowledge, and obedience. How do you handle failure? What are some ways in which you obsess about being perfect? How do you learn from failure and continue to grow in obedience?

7. God uses Examples to reach Unbelievers through acceptance, love, service, and friendship. This is made possible by the Example's lifestyle. Discuss some of the ways in which your life provides an example to others. How do you go about befriending Unbelievers and loving and serving them in Christ?

SESSION 5: THE LIFE OF THE TEACHER

Teachers don't merely provide information; they provide information in the needed context. Because a Teacher is first an Example, his or her life is the context for teaching God's truth. Becoming a Teacher is the fourth level of maturity as you continue growing in Christlikeness.

For Discussion

1. As you move from Example to Teacher, new Believers will naturally gravitate toward you. They need to be established in the faith, which includes learning the teachings of Scripture. Do you have a group of people who look to you for mentoring or discipling? Whom are you mentoring? Who is your mentor?

2. Believers have moved beyond the initial question of whether Christ is real and Christianity is true. They now seek answers to deeper spiritual questions and need guidance in living out their

faith. That is why they need the ministry of a Teacher. What are the characteristics of a good Teacher? In what ways do you see those characteristics in your life or in the life of your Teacher?

3. The call to teach is really a call to serve others. In what ways did Jesus model the servant-teacher lifestyle? What individuals modeled that lifestyle for you? How can you model the servant-teacher lifestyle for new Believers you know?

4. Because Teachers are looked up to and sought out for their knowledge and maturity, a major trap for Teachers is to give in to pride and arrogance. It is necessary for a Teacher to always approach his or her ministry as a servant. Jesus said the greatest among His followers is the servant of all, and the person who is first is the one who is last and least. (Read Mark 9:35; Luke 9:48.) It's not easy to be a servant to others. Share a few of your struggles in this area.

5. A Teacher is not a preacher, speaker, or presenter. There is a place for those ministries, but a Teacher is much more than that. Teachers are mentors and disciplers of others. Jesus spent three years training twelve men to carry out His work on earth after He ascended to the Father. To be effective, a Teacher must continue growing in Christlikeness as he or she is training others. How do you maintain your walk with Christ as you do the work of teaching others?

SESSION 6: THE LIFE OF THE IMPARTER

Imparters are called and chosen by God, and not every Christian enters this fifth stage of spiritual maturity. God is present in the ministry of Imparters in supernatural ways. Like Elijah, Elisha, and the apostles in the first century, Imparters speak for God. That level of maturity comes from a life that is constantly and consistently listening to God and obeying His voice.

For Discussion

1. The story of the prophet Elijah is told in 1 Kings 17–19. Before your group meets for session 6, take a moment to read those three chapters. Write down the miraculous events in Elijah's life that stand out the most to you. With your group, discuss modern-day examples of similar servants of God. Do you believe Elijah was unique, or could another believer carry out a similar ministry today?

2. *The Walk* suggests that Elijah had power from God that, in part, was subject to Elijah's control. For example, when he confronted the prophets of Baal, he set up a demonstration of God's miraculous power without first consulting God (see 1 Kings 18:22–39). Can you think of examples of a similar exercise of God's power in the life of New Testament believers? (Note, for example, Peter in Acts 5:4–9.)

3. The temptation to succumb to what Shaun calls "Gold, Glory, and Girls (or Gents)" is the temptation to yield to financial gain, pride, and lust. Can you think of individuals who reached the Imparter level of spiritual maturity only to fall victim to one or more of these temptations? Can you think of individuals who overcame and persevered, resisting the lure of these temptations? Why do you think one person was able to resist falling victim while another gave in? What made the difference between victory and defeat?

4. Fear confronts everyone at every level of spiritual maturity. Why is fear so debilitating? Can you think of examples from

Scripture where people in leadership roles yielded to fear? What
were the consequences?

5. Fear limits your ability to minister to others. How can you
    combat fear? What weapons does Scripture give you to use in
    overcoming fear?

SESSION 7: WALKING THE WALK EVERY DAY

Walking the Walk every day of your life is as simple as taking one step at
a time. In each of the stages, God will prepare you for the next. To reach
the fullness of maturity in Christ, you cannot skip a stage. If you jump
ahead, you will fail to learn essential lessons and character development
in the stage you skipped. This will present stumbling blocks in the later
stages. So take the stages in order, and allow God to grow your faith, character, and ministry at His pace.

For Discussion

1. God's order puts the right person in the right place at the right
    time. In chapter 14, Shaun refers to the example of Ananias
    praying for Paul to receive his sight (see Acts 9:1–19). Discuss
    other examples from Scripture in which a person heard from
    God and responded in a way that put the person in the right
    place at exactly the right time.

2. When we learn to listen to the Holy Spirit, we can hear Him
    urging us to take a particular action at a particular time. Have
    you ever heard His voice guiding you with that kind of speci-
    ficity? If so, tell the group about it.

3. Listening to God and following His orderly plan for your life
    can protect you from pitfalls you might otherwise encounter.
    Listening to God also opens the door to opportunities you

might otherwise miss. Share a few ways that following God's order in your life has protected you. Also talk about some of the opportunities it has opened for you.

4. We often judge our spiritual condition by how we feel, but God's voice and His work in our lives do not depend on our emotions. Share about a time when God spoke to you even when you didn't feel like He was close. Or share a time when you experienced His miraculous presence even when you didn't think you deserved it.

5. Christians at every level of maturity are called to live in relationship with one another. From Unbeliever to Imparter, we all are exhorted to remain accountable to others. To whom are you spiritually accountable, not in theory, but in a regular, ongoing relationship? How does accountability help you overcome the challenges and avoid the traps of the Walk to spiritual maturity?

6. After reading this book, you should have a sense of where you fall in the five stages of spiritual maturity. In which stage do you see yourself? Do the people in your discussion group share your assessment? Why or why not? Are there steps you need to take to align your life with God's order in this stage of the Walk?

A FINAL THOUGHT FROM SHAUN ALEXANDER

A young man I mentored all through his high school years left home for college looking like a weapon for God's Kingdom. He knew Scripture. He was obedient to God. He was an athlete and was very funny and popular. He finished his freshman year of college as he had ended his high school years—as a strong witness for the Lord. But by the end of his sophomore year, he was no longer the same kid. He had been fulfilling as many desires of the flesh as you could imagine.

He woke up one morning and texted me for the first time in a year: "I let you down."

I responded: "Little bro, I let you down. Number one, somehow I taught you to live moral for me instead of to honor Jesus. I am not your savior. I am nothing more than a messenger, a servant sending a message. Number two, I taught you the Word and how to obey it. I helped make Christianity fun and even cool. But I didn't teach you to fall *in love* with Jesus. Only a love affair with Jesus will sustain you and help you walk the Walk."

God's love for you is new every morning. Love is the fuel for the Walk, so fall in love with Jesus. Right now, start a love affair with the Savior.

Final question
Are you in a love affair with Jesus? Explain your love affair.

Notes

Chapter 1: The Walk

1. In 2005 I was credited with three NFL records and two team records with the Seattle Seahawks. The league records are for the running back who gained 1,000 yards in the fewest number of games (nine games). The second NFL record is for the most combined touchdowns in a regular season (twenty-eight). The third league record is for the most rushing touchdowns in a regular season (twenty-seven). The two team records with the Seahawks are for the most 100-yard games (eleven) and for the most yards gained in one season (1,880).

2. The book was Rick Joyner's *The Call* (Fort Mill, SC: MorningStar Publications, 1999). It is a companion to Rick Joyner, *The Final Quest* (Fort Mill, SC: MorningStar Publications, 1996).

3. Before the football season begins, teams conduct intensive training camps. During those camps players train in two sessions each day: one in the morning and one in the afternoon. Held during the hottest part of the summer, two-a-days are grueling, hot, and nasty.

4. *The Last Dragon* stars Taimak as Leroy Green. It was produced by Berry Gordy, Rupert Hitzig, and Joseph M. Caracciolo, directed by Michael Schultz, written by Louis Venosta, and released in 1985 by TriStar Pictures.

Chapter 3: Trials, Traps, and Victories

1. Humanity was created in God's image. We have free will to make choices. We also have power, albeit limited power, which gives us

the capacity to do good or evil. Our character restrains and
guides the use of our power.

2. C. S. Lewis, *Surprised by Joy: The Shape of My Early Life* (New
York: Harcourt Brace, 1955), 56.

3. Lewis, *Surprised by Joy,* 57.

Chapter 4: Peter Walks into Real Belief

1. For a discussion of messianic hope and expectation, see Colin
Brown, ed., *The New International Dictionary of New Testament
Theology,* 4 vols. (Grand Rapids: Zondervan, 1986), 2:334ff. See
also Charles Guignebert, *The Jewish World in the Time of Jesus*
(London: Kegan, Pascal, Trench, Trubner, 1939).

Chapter 5: Life as a Believer

1. Philippe Petit was born in France in 1949. He performed numerous high-wire shows and became known for walking between
notable structures, including the towers of Notre Dame de Paris,
the Niagara River, and the Sydney Harbor Bridge in Sydney,
Australia.

Chapter 8: Becoming an Example

1. Genesis 1:31, author's paraphrase. Throughout the creation nar-
rative, God indicates that what He created is good.

Chapter 12: Trials, Traps and Victories

1. In the Bible, the word *overseer* is sometimes translated "bishop."

2. Crenshaw Christian Center, 7901 South Vermont Avenue, Los
Angeles, California, was founded by Dr. Frederick K. C. Price Sr.
and is currently located on a site previously occupied by Pepper-

dine University's Los Angeles campus. For more information about the church, see www.crenshawchristiancenter.net.

3. Saddleback Church has five campuses throughout Southern California. The church's primary facility is in Lake Forest, California. For more about the church, see www.saddleback.com.

4. Rick Warren, *The Purpose Driven Life: What on Earth Am I Here For?* (Grand Rapids: Zondervan, 2002).

5. Walt Kallestad has written more than twenty books, many of them inspired by his experiences as a pastor. Community Church of Joy is located at 21000 North 75th Avenue, Glendale, Arizona. For more information about the church, see www.joyonline.org.

6. The Dream Center is a twenty-four-hour church. Its primary facility is located at 2301 Bellevue Avenue, Los Angeles, California. The church has a number of other campuses and ministry locations in and around Los Angeles and in New York. For more information about the church, see www.dreamcenter.org.

Chapter 14: Called to Be an Imparter

1. For more information about Heidi Baker and Iris Ministries, see www.irismin.org or www.irisministries.com.

Chapter 18: The Year God Gave Me Nine Cities

1. The Senior Bowl is an annual college football all-star game played in Mobile on the weekend before the NFL's Super Bowl.

ACKNOWLEDGMENTS

To my bride, Valerie;
our three little girls, Heaven, Trinity, and Eden;
and our son, Joseph Prince.
Thanks for love and life and laughs.

To everybody I have met on my journey.
Jesus is God, and there is nothing greater than Him.
Thanks for being a part of my walk.

ALSO BY SHAUN ALEXANDER

*Touchdown Alexander: My Story of Faith,
Football, and Pursuing the Dream*

For more information about Shaun Alexander
visit www.shaunalexander.com

052285427